THE *Best* OF

JAMES W. MOORE

Thoughts on Faith and Grace from a Master Storyteller

Abingdon Press
Nashville

THE BEST OF JAMES W. MOORE
THOUGHTS ON FAITH AND GRACE FROM A MASTER STORYTELLER

Library of Congress Cataloging-in-Publication Data has been requested.

ISBN 978-1-4267-4200-2

12 13 14 15 16 17 18 19 20 21—10 9 8 7 6 5 4 3 2 1

MANUFACTURED IN THE UNITED STATES OF AMERICA

CONTENTS

PREFACE

The Bible is all about stories. Close your eyes, open it up, and put your finger down on the page, and you will likely be pointing to a story. Within the pages of Scripture you'll find big stories, like how God created the world, or delivered the Hebrew people from slavery in Egypt; small stories, like Jesus blessing a group of children; funny stories, like Jonah pouting because the plant that was giving him shade had died; sad stories, like the rich young ruler turning his back on Jesus because he couldn't accept Jesus' invitation to "sell everything you own and distribute the money to the poor...and come, follow me" (Luke 18:22, CEB); exciting stories, like Elijah vs. the four hundred prophets of Baal on Mt. Carmel; inspiring stories, like Paul's encounter with the resurrected Christ on the road to Damascus; and, most importantly, the overarching story of God's refusal to give up on sinful humanity, accepting even death on a cross to show us just how much God loves us, and wants to save us. Yes, it seems that God's got a thing for stories.

Perhaps that explains why James W. Moore is such an effective witness to the gospel; he, too, has a thing for stories. Drawing on stories from his own life, from the daily headlines, from books and movies, and especially from the Bible, Dr. Moore weaves together an uplifting and hopeful tale about God's love for you and me in Jesus Christ. His stories take us down country lanes and up city streets, into the homes and hearts of people who have been sought and found by God's redeeming grace. Often funny, always thought-provoking, his writing brings us back time and again to the biblical truth that God's story is still going on, that we have a chapter in it, and more than anything God wants that chapter to have a happy ending.

This book brings together some of the best of James W. Moore's stories and insights about life spent in the presence of God. May they touch your heart as they have the hearts of all who have encountered them before.

—*The Editors*

CHAPTER ONE

STORIES OF GETTING
IT WRONG

Our problem is that we settle for too little. We stop reaching, stop growing. We accept "childish" religion rather than paying the price for "mature" faith. We are content with a "Chopsticks" faith in a Beethoven world. Let me tell you what I mean.

Some years ago I had an interesting experience at a party. There was a house full of people, a festive mood, much noise, a hubbub of conversation, and party sounds. People were standing in little clusters, and talking. Others were playing games, listening to records, watching television, or preparing refreshments in the kitchen.

In the midst of all this, I sat down at the piano, flexed my two index fingers, and began to play "Chopsticks"—which just happens to be my complete repertoire of piano selections.

After a bit, a close friend walked over, tapped me on the shoulder, and said with a grin, "Jim, why don't you get up and let somebody play the piano who knows what she is doing?" I stood up, and he introduced a young woman who was visiting our city from another state. After some coaxing, she sat down and began to play. She was magnificent! She became one with that musical instrument. Her hands moved gracefully and confidently up and down the keyboard as she played a Beethoven masterpiece.

She was so good that everybody in the house literally dropped what they were doing. Conversation stopped, table games were pushed aside, the television was turned off, people came out of the kitchen. Everybody gathered to listen. When she finished, there was a kind of reverent silence for a brief moment... and then spontaneous, thunderous applause as we called for more.

Out of that experience, I had several thoughts. Was that the same piano I had been playing only moments before? What was the difference? Well, it was clear that my feeble attempt was childish, amateurish, and simplistic, while hers was studied, disciplined, dedicated, loving, masterful. Also, I had contented myself with using only two fingers and eight notes, whereas she used all her fingers and all the notes. The truth is that I had settled for just a little musical knowledge; she had obviously committed her life to it. She had trained, sacrificed, practiced, learned, and as a result had become a mature master musician.

On a deeper level, there is an interesting parallel in the world of faith. In our spiritual pilgrimage, too many of us fail to really apply ourselves. We quit too early, settle for too little. We have a "Chopsticks" faith when we could have so much more. In our world today there are too many immature people and too many childish actions. I am concerned about this because I believe that childishness causes much of the misery in the world today. Friendships are destroyed, marriages disrupted, churches split, families polarized, wars started, lives lost, hearts broken—all due to spiritual and emotional childishness

It happened at recess at an elementary school. Tom bumped into Jack and knocked Jack down. It made Jack so mad that he was determined to get Tom back. All day long, Jack plotted his revenge. Finally, he decided to find a rock and carry it in his pocket, and the next time he saw Tom he would hit him with it. That would teach Tom a lesson. Jack was proud of his plan. Early the next morning, Jack found the perfect rock. It was rough and jagged, just what he needed. He put it in the front right pocket of his jeans and went off to school looking for Tom so he could get his revenge. But Tom had the flu and didn't make it to school that day. For every day the rest of that week, Jack carried the rock in his right front pocket, but Tom was still not in school. Then on Friday night, as he prepared to go to bed, Jack took off his jeans only to discover that his leg was bruised and scraped and bleeding. The jagged rock, the weapon of vengeance he had carried in his pocket all week, had injured him! That's the way vengeance works. It hurts us more than it hurts others. The vengeful, unforgiving, hateful spirit is so destructive and so dangerous and so un-Christian.

Some months ago a young man showed up at the church. A year or so before, he had gotten into trouble with drugs. There had been a tough confrontation with his father, a heated argument, harsh words were spoken, and in a rage, this young man had run away from home. Last Christmas he went back home, but he didn't go into the house. He stood outside in the snow and looked in the window. He saw his family having Christmas dinner before the fireplace. He wanted to go in. He wanted to be back in the family circle, but his pride, his embarrassment, kept him out in the cold. He knew his parents had been trying to find him, but he just could not bring himself to say, "I'm sorry."

Upon hearing this story, I said to him, "Let's call them right now. I have an idea they will welcome you with open arms."

He was hesitant, but finally agreed and gave me the number. But as I began to dial, he got cold feet.

"Wait a minute," he said. "Let me think about it overnight." He told me he had a place to stay and that he would come back in the morning. When he left, I wondered if I would ever see him again.

Well, I did see him, but not in my office. I saw him that evening—hitchhiking—holding a sign that read "New Orleans." I had a sad feeling deep down in my soul. Here was a young man running away from forgiveness, running away from a bright future, running away from his family—*trapped, paralyzed, shackled* in a prison of his own making, a prison constructed of pride and the fear of embarrassment.

I wonder how many people today are imprisoned like that. How many want to set something right? How many want to make a profession of faith for the first time, or ask for forgiveness, or make a new start. And yet, because of pride or fear of embarrassment, they turn away sorrowfully.

Pride is a spiritual virus that will devastate your soul. Now, let me hurry to say that there is a good kind of pride. We all know that. It's good to be a proud American. It's good to be proud of your state, your school, your church, your heritage, your family.

But that's not the kind of pride Jesus is talking about in the Sermon on the Mount. He is exposing here that unhealthy pride, pride that is arrogant and pompous and haughty. The holier-than-thou pride—pride that shouts to the world, "I'm better than you," pride that is conceited, pretentious, and puffed up. That kind of pride is dangerous and so destructive—and it will so quickly poison your soul.

Remember how Jesus put it: "Beware of practicing your piety before men in order to be seen by them." And, "When you give alms, sound no trumpet before you." And, "When you pray do not show off. Do not stand on street corners offering up empty phrases, trying to impress people with your many words."

Jesus had chosen for himself the way of the suffering servant, the humble, self-giving Savior, and therefore he would not be impressed with "religious show-offs." He saw that kind of arrogant pride as a dramatic symbol of "soul sickness."

A seasoned senior angel was giving a brand-new freshman angel a tour of the heavens. The freshman angel was wide-eyed and awestruck as he saw the vastness and majesty and wonder of God's incredible universe. When they came to the Milky Way, the mature senior angel said to the freshman angel, "Come over here, son, I want to show you something special. Look down there! That tiny planet is called Earth. It looks rather insignificant from here, doesn't it? It looks so small and so inconsequential, but something quite remarkable happened there some years ago. You see, the people of Earth had gotten off the track a bit. They were missing the whole point of their existence. They were missing the meaning of life. So God sent his only Son into that world to save the people and to teach them what God meant life to be for them on Earth."

"Wow! That's amazing!" said the freshman angel excitedly. "You mean to tell me that God's Son actually visited that little planet? How pleased the people of Earth must have been to receive him! I can just imagine that they must have had a great celebration for him on Earth."

"No," said the senior angel quietly. Then, with tears glistening in his eyes, he said, "No—they tried to kill him! They were so wrapped up in their old, rigid ways of doing things that when God's Son presented some new ideas, they resented him, and they tried to silence him. Blinded by the old, they missed the new. Surely the Lord was in that place, and they did not know it. God was there, and they were out to lunch!"

How easy it is to fall into this trap! How easy it is to become so paralyzed by our usual ways of doing things that new ways threaten the life out of us! How easy it is to become so closed minded that we are blind to any kind of new truth! Blinded by the forms, we miss the force! Blinded by our rituals, we miss our reason for being! Blinded by our narrowness, we miss God's nearness. Blinded by the old, we miss the new!

There is an old story about a major league baseball manager who needed some help for his team as they were in the thick of a heated pennant race. He sent his best scout down to the minor leagues to find a good hitter. The next day the scout called back and he was so excited he could hardly speak. "I've found just the player we need," he said. "He's terrific! With this guy, we can win the World Series! It's unbelievable how good he is! He could come to the major leagues today and become an instant star! He is without question the best baseball player I have ever seen!" The manager said, "Can he hit?" "Well, no," answered the scout. "He's a pitcher. But he pitched a perfect game. Every pitch was in the strike zone. He didn't walk anybody. He struck out every hitter—a no-hitter, a perfect game! In fact, only one player on the other team touched the ball with the bat, and that was a foul tip!" The manager said, "Forget about the pitcher! Hire the guy who fouled one off. What we need is a hitter!"

Well, the point is clear—the narrow view blinds us to new possibilities. The manager had it in his mind that the only way to help his team was with a new hitter, and blinded by that narrow view, he missed the greatest player of all time! Narrowness is a spiritual cataract because it blinds us to new opportunities, new possibilities, new truths, and new ways.

I have a friend who once told of a strange idea he had as a boy: he thought that he could outrun germs! Once, as a little boy, he came down with a terrible cold, and somehow he got the idea that if he could run fast from one room to another, he could run away from those germs the way he could run away from his puppy.

His mother found him dashing from room to room, all out of breath, and when she discovered what he was attempting to do, she gently but wisely called him back to reality. She explained that he couldn't outrun the germs; no matter where he ran or how fast he went the germs would go with him. "The sooner you quit trying to run away from your cold," she said, "and start doing what the doctor prescribed, the quicker you will get well."

There is a great truth here, not only for treating colds, but also for dealing with all of life's problems; and yet we are so slow to learn that! We can't outrun our problems. The sooner we accept this fact and decide to face our problems, the better; and yet we are so slow to understand that. This incessant search for a way to escape the inescapable and the chronic resentment of the problems are an incredible waste of energy. And yet, if we are honest, we must confess that we have squandered a large portion of our lives running, hiding, fleeing, and escaping.

Some scholars have referred to our time as "the Age of Escapism." The reference may be indeed appropriate. Look at what is happening. For example, we've seen an increase in drug abuse. Now, let me ask you something. Why do people take drugs? Why do people use and abuse drugs?

Some people use drugs to "get high"—in other words, to get above and beyond their problems; but they ultimately crash, with more trouble than they started with in the first place. Some people take drugs so they can sleep, because if they can sleep then they can avoid their problems at least for a little while; but when they wake up, the problems are still there. Some people take drugs so they can relax, in the hope that somehow the tension might be released or eased; but still again, the tension returns, the uptightness comes back, the nerves stretch tighter—and sometimes they snap. Some people take drugs so they can get drunk. (Don't forget that alcohol is a drug.) They drink and drink and get drunk so they can forget their problems; but when they sober up, the troubles are still there, along with a terrific hangover. Some people take drugs so they can cope with life's problems. They say, "This pill will make me brave"; "This pill will calm me down"; "This pill will give me strength"; "This pill will settle my nerves."

And it's all so ridiculous. It's all so absurd. All of these abuses and misuses of drugs are simply our childish attempts to outrun the germs, our infantile ways of trying to run away from or hide from our problems. But when will we ever learn that there is no escape from the problems of this world? Problems are here to stay. There are no problem-free jobs. There are no problem-free marriages. There are no problem-free homes. There are no problem-free communities. There are no problem-free churches. There are no problem-free worlds.

So, we really can't run away. We really can't escape. We have to face the problems; handle the difficulties; deal with the troubles. There is no hiding place. There is no place to run!

So we need to learn how to cope with our hardships creatively, productively, and meaningfully. Once again, our great teacher is Jesus. We see in him the model and the pattern for dealing with problems productively. In him, we see how to cope with difficulties in creative ways.

Have you ever heard of the utopian complex? It's a term used by psychologists and psychiatrists to describe people who go through life looking for the perfect situation and waiting for the perfect moment to do what they ought to do and to be what they ought to be. Meanwhile, life passes them by and they end up feeling frustrated and betrayed and empty and miserable. Let me illustrate this with a story.

In the early days of our country, a Native American princess went one morning to visit a neighboring tribe. The tribe she visited was known far and wide for their magnificent cornfields. The corn they produced each harvest was simply marvelous—without equal! No other tribe even came close. The princess asked if she might select one ear of corn from their field to take home and provide seed corn for her own tribe's fields the next year.

Graciously, her request was granted, but there was one condition. She would have to make her choice as she walked down the row! That is, she could not turn back and pick an ear of corn she had already passed by. So off she went, walking slowly down the row looking intently for that one perfect ear of corn. She walked and looked and pondered and studied, but she could not bring herself to pick an ear of corn for fear that there might just be a better one farther down the row.

All of a sudden she stepped out of the field and she realized what she had done. It hit her with a sickening thud! She had blown her opportunity! She had walked down the entire length of the row and still had not found that one absolutely perfect ear of corn. There was no turning back. Sadly, she had walked out of the field without making a choice, and so she went home empty-handed!

What a great parable this is for each one of us. Each day that we have is a gracious and generous gift from God. Each day provides us with many opportunities that will never come again. If you wait to select the perfect opportunity, you may miss the one opportunity that will benefit you the most. If you wait until that perfect date comes along, you may never go out. If you wait to join the one perfect cause in life, you may never contribute to anything. If you wait till you find the perfect job, you will be unemployed. If you delay participation in the spiritual life until things are just right, or until you think you are worthy, then you will miss out on life and faith and God. If you spend your life trapped in the utopian complex, looking for that perfect situation and waiting for that perfect moment to do what you know you ought to do, and to be what you know you ought to be, you may well discover too late that life has passed you by.

Like the Native American princess, you will have walked out of the cornfield frustrated—you will have ended up empty-handed.

I'm thinking of a man I know in another state who is a fine singer. He has an excellent tenor voice, but he has not sung in church for more than thirty years. Thirty-three years ago, he was active in his church's music program, sang in the choir, and was the church's main soloist.

But then a new singer moved to town. The choir director graciously invited the newcomer to sing a solo, and the new singer did well. The main soloist couldn't stand it. He couldn't bear to hear people compliment the new singer, so he quit the choir.

The choir suffered his loss for a while, but soon enough, others took up the slack. None of us is indispensable; the church rolls on.

But that man has sulked and seethed and buried his talent for thirty-three years. He doesn't come to church much anymore, and when he does come, he sits in the congregation with bitterness written all over his face.

He is mad most of the time. He is cynical and critical of the church, especially the music program, but people long ago stopped listening to him. Here is a man who has wasted his talent and who has wasted thirty-three years. Think of what he has missed while making himself miserable—all because he was afraid he wouldn't do as well as others.

That kind of fear leads to bitterness, self-pity, jealousy, envy, and resentment. That kind of fear is so debilitating and so unnecessary. We don't have to outdo other people. All God asks is that we be the best we can be.

Have you heard the story about the woman who was to bake a cake for the church ladies' bake sale but forgot to do it until the last minute? Alice was her name. She baked an angel food cake. But when she took it out of the oven, the center had dropped flat. It was too late to bake another cake, so she looked around the house for something to build up the center of the cake. Alice found it in the bathroom—a roll of toilet paper. She plunked it in and covered it with beautiful, luscious icing. The finished product looked elegant and sumptuous, so she rushed it to the church.

Alice then gave her daughter some money and asked her to be at the bake sale the minute the doors opened and buy the cake and bring it straight home. But when the daughter arrived at the bake sale, the attractive cake had already been sold. Alice was beside herself.

A couple of days later, Alice was invited to a friend's home for a festive party. A fancy lunch was served, and to top it off, the cake in question was presented for dessert. When Alice saw the notorious cake, she started to get out of her chair to rush into the kitchen to tell her hostess all about it. But before she could get to her feet, one of the other ladies said, "What a beautiful cake!" to which the hostess said, "Thank you; I baked it myself!" At this point, Alice sat back in her chair just to watch what would happen next!

Well, there's a sermon there somewhere, and it's about how our mixed-up priorities and our haughty pride can come back to haunt us, and when that happens, it is indeed sorrowful.

Some years ago, in a small town in central Europe, a visitor saw something that fascinated him, something that seemed very strange to him. He noticed the native villagers performing the same highly unusual ritual. As they passed by a certain ordinary-looking wall, they would nod casually in the direction of the wall and then make the sign of the cross as they walked on by.

Some would be walking briskly, others more slowly, but they all did the same thing: they would nod at the wall and then make the sign of the cross as they passed by. When the visitor asked why they did this, no one knew. "We've always done that," they said. "It's a tradition, a time-honored ritual in our village. Everybody does it. Always have."

The visitor's curiosity got the best of him and he began chipping away at the layers of paint and dirt covering the wall until, underneath, he discovered a magnificent mural of Mary and the baby Jesus! Generations before, the townspeople had had a beautiful reason for bowing and making the sign of the cross at that place. It had been an altar of prayer in the heart of the village.

But succeeding generations didn't know that; they had only learned the ritual. They continued to go through the motions without knowing the reason. They performed the practice, but it had absolutely no meaning for them and had no impact on their lives at all. That's an appropriate parable for many people today in their approach to religion, isn't it?

Their faith experience is not much more than a vague nod in God's direction. They casually perform some of the rituals of faith, but they don't really know why, and the rituals have become so routine, so casual, so matter-of-fact, that there is no power, no strength, no inspiration in them at all—a little nod here, a token gesture there, but no depth, no spirit, no life!

But in the Sermon on the Mount Jesus shows us dramatically that this kind of shallow, nonchalant approach to faith won't work. There are storms ahead; the rains of trouble will fall; the floods of stress will come; the winds of challenge will lash against us. Shaky, unstable, wobbly, wavering, casual, routine faith won't hold together. The storms of life will rip that apart and smash it to the ground. We need a strong and stable house of faith built on a rock-solid foundation!

CHAPTER TWO

STORIES OF CARING
AND COMPASSION

At a national coaches conference some years ago, a famous coach was the guest speaker. He spoke on the subject of how important it is to encourage one another. He told of a game back in the late 1970s.

Going into the season the team was confident. They had great talent, especially at quarterback, where the team had three players who were about equal.

Before the season, the second-string quarterback got hurt and was going to be out for the season. Coach felt sorry for the young man, but he thought, *We will be OK because we've got two more.*

However, in a game on a sunny Saturday afternoon, the first-string quarterback got badly hurt. Confidently, Coach sent in the third-string quarterback—after all, he thought, there is not much difference between the three quarterbacks in talent and experience. But a few plays later, he too got injured in the game.

Coach didn't know what to do. The fourth-string quarterback was a senior; in four years he had never been in a game, not one play, but the coach had no other choice, so he called for him.

Meanwhile, out on field, the team's all-star running back had gathered the other ten players into a huddle, and he said to them:

"Fellows, we are in big trouble here. I don't know who Coach is going to send in. But, whoever it is, we have got to make him feel like he is the best quarterback in America. We have got to make him feel like he is the man of the hour and this is his moment. We have got to make him feel like we believe in him, we trust him, and we know he can do it!"

So, when that fourth-string senior quarterback (who had never played a down) started onto the field, there was fear in his eyes, but it didn't last long. The offensive team ran to meet him. They hugged him. They patted him on the back. They told him they were ready and that they believed in him. They pumped him up so much that they not only won that game but all the rest and they won the conference championship with an 11-0 record!

There we see it: the power of encouragement. We in the church should be first and foremost the sons and daughters of encouragement.

<hr/>

Have you heard the story about the small girl, not more than ten or eleven years old, who was standing in a soup kitchen line in a poverty-stricken section of a large city? She was the last one in the long line. Many people had shown up that day, quite a few more than usual. The volunteers preparing and serving the food that day realized that the food was starting to run short. The servers were concerned.

The little girl did not seem to notice. Her attention was focused on three small children who were across the street, sitting and waiting for her in the shade under a big oak tree. The little girl continued to wait patiently in line that day, but when she finally made it to the servers, the only thing left was one banana. Without complaint, she took the single banana joyfully. With a smile and a nod, she thanked the volunteer servers, and then she walked back across the street to join the three smaller children.

Were they her siblings? Were they her friends? We don't know that, but what we do know is what the little girl did. Carefully, she peeled the banana. She broke it into three equal pieces, and she gave each of the other children one-third of the banana. Then she sat down on the curb and licked the inside of the banana peel. A bystander who happened to witness that little girl's act of sacrificial love said later, "When I saw what that little girl did that day, I saw the face of God."

Christian love is self-giving and sacrificial. It means to give yourself to other people. It means to go out on a limb for others. Christian love is not just something you feel. It's something you do for the sake of others. Bartimaeus was crying for help. Jesus knew his need and came to the rescue.

Have you heard about a little twelve-year-old African boy who lived with his family in a small village? His name was Lawi. One day as Lawi was baby-sitting with his little brother while the other members of the family were at work in the sugarcane fields, their little hut caught fire and was quickly enveloped in flames. Lawi was outside, but remembering his little brother, he jumped up and ran into the blazing hut, only to find the baby trapped by a burning rafter which had fallen on him. Hurriedly, Lawi worked to free his brother. He had trouble getting him loose as the flames danced about his head. Finally, he freed him. He picked him up, carried him outside, and revived him just as the hut caved in.

By this time the villagers had gathered outside the smoldering remains. They had been too frightened to go inside or do anything to help, and they were tremendously impressed with the courage of young Lawi.

They congratulated him for his heroic efforts: "Lawi, you are very brave. Weren't you frightened? What were you thinking as you ran into the burning hut?"

Lawi answered, "I wasn't thinking of anything. I just heard my little brother crying!"

How long has it been since you heard your brother or sister crying? How long has it been since you stopped and did something about it?

Richard Nixon was the thirty-sixth Vice President of the United States and the thirty-seventh President of the United States. He is the only man to have been elected twice to the vice presidency and twice to the presidency.

However, he may always be remembered as being the only U.S. President to have resigned from office. His resignation, of course, came in response to the complex of scandals referred to as Watergate.

A few years after his resignation, Richard Nixon came back to Washington, D.C., to attend the funeral of Hubert Humphrey, the man Nixon had defeated in the presidential election of 1968. The holding room in the church was packed with powerful political dignitaries, but one man, Richard Nixon, stood alone against a wall. Even though he had received a full pardon from his successor, President Gerald Ford, Nixon was still seen by many people as political poison, so they all shunned him. No one spoke to him. No one looked at him. No one acknowledged him.

It was Nixon's first visit back to our nation's capital since that dark, fateful day when he departed the White House in a Marine helicopter, but now he stood there alone.

But then President Jimmy Carter entered the building. He greeted friends and colleagues warmly. President Carter saw Richard Nixon standing off in the distance, all alone. He realized what was happening.

President Carter's heart went out to Richard Nixon. Immediately, in full view of everyone, President Carter walked straight over to Richard Nixon. He took his hand, he embraced him, and then, loud enough for all to hear, President Carter said to former President Richard Nixon, "Welcome home, Mr. President! Welcome home!"

That simple act of compassion was a turning point for Richard Nixon and, in a way, for our nation, because it allowed Richard Nixon to regain some of his stature as an elder statesman, and it paved the way for both Democratic and Republican successors to the presidency to consult with Nixon regarding foreign policy.

Now, I'm sure that there were some there that day who criticized President Carter for welcoming Nixon back so warmly, but somewhere in heaven God was smiling, because our God is loving, merciful, forgiving, and compassionate, and he wants us to be that way too. And the truth is that we all are welcomed into the family of God only because of God's extravagant generosity and grace and forgiveness and compassion in Jesus Christ.

As Christians, we are first and last called to be servants of God. We are not called to be prima donnas or celebrities or superstars. We are called to be humble, willing, self-giving servants of Christ.

Some years ago, a Christian Ashram was started in India. Converts would come there to learn the Christian faith. One convert who came to the Ashram was a Brahmin. You remember that the Brahmins were the upper class, the upper crust of society.

In this Christian Ashram, everyone present was expected to help with the community chores—to mop the floors, to wash the dishes, to serve the meals, even to clean the bathhouses. The former Brahmin came to the Ashram leader one day and announced that he could not possibly perform such menial chores. They were beneath him, he said. The Ashram leader told him that in Christ there are no menial tasks and that all good works are sacred, and that he should have no trouble as a Christian mopping floors and washing dishes and even cleaning bathhouses. When the Brahmin heard that, he said to the leader, "I'm converted, but not that far!"

Put that over against Mother Teresa, who simply pretended that every person she met was Christ in disguise. She served every person and performed every task as if she were doing it for Christ. And that's what it really means to be a servant Christian.

I once saw a painting in which the artist depicts an old Chinese legend about heaven and hell. On one side of the painting, hell is portrayed. It shows a group of people seated at a great table with a sumptuous feast before them. But the people are miserable. They can't eat the magnificent feast because their chopsticks are longer than their arms. They can't get the food to their mouths. So they sit there starving, their faces drawn with hunger and self-pity.

Next to that picture is a picture of heaven. It depicts the same people, the same banquet, the same long chopsticks.

There is only one subtle and significant difference. The people in the heaven picture are radiantly happy. Their faces are vibrant with joy because they are *feeding each other*! They are reaching across the table with the long chopsticks and feeding the persons seated across from them.

The point of this ancient legend is precisely the point I want to make—the difference between heaven and hell is self-centeredness. Hell is symbolized by self-centeredness and self-pity, heaven is symbolized by self-giving and sharing. Self-centeredness is shaky sand—a poor foundation for these stormy times. But self-giving love is a rock—a firm foundation for the living of these days. So let the storms rage, let the rains fall, let the winds blow and beat upon our house. It will not fall if it is built on self-giving.

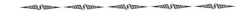

There was a *Peanuts* cartoon where Lucy decides that Linus, her little brother, needs to give up his security blanket. So while Linus is taking his afternoon nap, she slips his blanket away from him, takes it outside, and buries it in the ground. When Linus wakes up and realizes that his security blanket is gone, he goes into a mind-boggling panic attack. He can't breathe. He screams that he has to have that blanket, that he can't live without that blanket. Snoopy walks by and he sees Linus's big problem and Snoopy comes to the rescue! Snoopy rushes outside and with his trusty nose sniffs around until he finds the blanket. He digs up the blanket and dashes back to return it to a grateful Linus. With one hand Linus grabs the blanket and with his other arm he hugs Snoopy and thanks him excitedly, telling Snoopy that Snoopy has saved his life!

Linus is elated, and he and Snoopy celebrate and dance for joy over his reunion with his spiritual tourniquet, his blanket. In the final scene, Snoopy is lying on his doghouse thinking this thought: "Every now and then my existence is justified!"

When do you feel most alive; when do you feel that your existence is justified? Isn't it when you are doing something worthwhile for someone else? When you love others more than yourself?

Some years ago when I was a seminary student, I served a church in a beautiful little village in Ohio. One summer afternoon, on the main street of that town, I drove into one of the most memorable experiences of my life.

19

It was raining steadily. Just ahead of me, a little girl, who looked to be about eight or nine years old, lost control of her bicycle on the rain-slick street and crashed to the pavement, scraping her knee and spilling a sack full of groceries in the street. I did what anyone would do. I stopped to help.

She cried quietly as I cleaned her injured knee and helped gather up the scattered groceries; then she willingly accepted my offer to drive her home. We deposited the soggy groceries in the back seat and placed her bike in the trunk. Following her directions, we arrived at her home in a few minutes. Her mother was most gracious and appreciative—until she found out who I was.

When I said I was the new minister in town, her mood changed abruptly. She became nervous, appeared almost frightened, and began to beg me to leave. She blurted out that her husband, who was due home any moment, didn't like ministers and would not permit them in the house. Early in life he evidently had some bad experience that had caused him to despise the church.

As his wife told me of his hostility, I noticed that on the wall were pictures of her husband as a champion boxer—a huge man with monstrous arms and fierce eyes. Even as I looked at his pictures and the trophies and ribbons displayed there, I too had a sudden mood change. I decided it probably would be a good idea for me to leave before he got home!

But it was too late. He was coming in the front door. Nervously, his wife stammered out an introduction.

As soon as he heard I was a minister, he glared at me. "Get out and don't come back. No one from the church is wanted here. No minister is welcome here. Get out right now!"

His wife looked at the floor, embarrassed, and I did what anyone in his right mind would do: I said, "I'm sorry" and left.

Next Sunday morning during the first hymn, I couldn't believe my eyes. That man slipped into the back of the church and took a seat on the last pew. A shocked murmur slid across the congregation, a few gasps, numerous whispers, lots of raised eyebrows. I gulped a couple of times myself. During the last hymn he slipped quietly out.

I didn't see him again until the next Sunday. He returned, and at the end of the service came to the altar and joined the church on profession of faith. It was a touching moment. People were moved to tears.

And I was moved to curiosity. Which sermon had touched him? This Sunday's, or the one before? What had broken through that hard shell of hostility? I had to know!

His answer caught me off guard. "I hate to tell you this, but it wasn't either of your sermons. It wasn't anything you said."

"Well, what was it?" I asked.

I'll never forget his answer: "You were kind to my little girl. That's what got my attention. You were kind to my daughter."

I learned a valuable lesson that day—a lesson about the importance of kindness. In fact, one of the most significant and impressive signs of Christian faith is kindness. We don't need to be thoughtless or arrogant or rude or harsh or preoccupied or hateful. We can choose to be kind. You see, we may master church history, speak high-sounding theological phrases, quote the great philosophers, even commit to memory large blocks of Scripture, but only when we show people genuine kindness do they really begin to see our faith.

A friend recently sent me a story about a mother who was preparing pancakes for her two sons one Saturday morning. Kevin and Ryan just loved pancakes. In fact, they loved their mom's pancakes so much that on this particular Saturday morning they began to argue (as brothers will do) over who would get the first pancake. Five-year-old Kevin and three-year-old Ryan were not only fussing; they were also pushing and shoving, trying, each one, to be first in line and get the first pancake.

Their mother saw the opportunity for a moral lesson, so she said, "Boys, boys! Calm down! I want to ask you a question. If Jesus were here with us this morning, what do you think he would say?" No answer. "Well," she continued, "I'll tell you what he would say. He would say, 'Please let my brother have the first pancake; I can wait.'"

In reply, five-year-old Kevin said, "Great idea, Mom!" and then he turned to his younger brother and said, "Ryan, *you* be Jesus!"

I love that story, not only because it's funny, but also because it is so typical of us. Most of us are convinced that the hard work of the gospel can and should be done, but we want somebody else to do it. We want great Sunday school classes for our children, our youth, and our adults, but we want somebody else to provide them. We want and expect to have a great choir, but we want somebody else to make it happen. We want somebody else to drive the bus for the youth, to look after the landscaping, to help the poor, to visit the sick, to go on the mission work trip. We want the Spirit of Christ to be alive and well and evident in our church, our city, our world, but we want somebody else to do the work of Christ. Like five-year-old Kevin, we say, "You be Jesus—not me!"

Without question, the hope for our world today is found in Jesus Christ and the love he embodied. He shows us what God is like and what God wants us to be like, and the word for it is love. We are all familiar with the name Babe Ruth. He was one of the greatest baseball players of all time. "The Babe," as he was affectionately called, hit 714 home runs during his baseball career. Unfortunately, he played too long. He continued to play when he had gotten older and his ability had waned, both at bat and in the field.

There's a story about how during one of his last games as a professional, the aging Babe Ruth had a terrible day. He made several errors. In just one inning, his errors were responsible for five runs scored by the opposing team. As Babe Ruth walked off the field after that disastrous inning and headed for the dugout, a crescendo of boos and catcalls was directed at him by the angry crowd. Babe Ruth had never known a moment like that. The fans who had loved him for so many years had turned on him with a vengeance. It was a painful and humiliating moment for this great athlete who had been the number one star of baseball for so long.

But just then, a little boy in the bleachers couldn't stand it. He couldn't bear seeing Babe Ruth hurt like that. The little boy jumped over the railing onto the playing field, and with tears streaming down his face, he ran toward Babe Ruth. He knelt before his hero and threw his arms around the player's legs. Babe Ruth picked the little boy up and hugged him tightly.

Suddenly, the noise from the stands came to an abrupt stop. There was no more booing. In fact, an incredible hush fell over the entire ballpark. The boy's love for Babe Ruth had melted the hearts of that hostile crowd. Love happened in right field, and suddenly the outcome of a baseball game didn't seem that important anymore.

Truth and love are fixed points in this changing world—fixed points we can always trust and always count on. They bring us back to reality.

Recently, I read a story about two men who were best friends. Bill and Tom had enjoyed each other's company since they were children. They had grown up together. They loved to hunt and fish. One Saturday morning, they went hunting, and there was an accident. As Bill was climbing over a barbed-wire fence, he fell, and his gun went off. He shot himself in the leg and began to bleed profusely.

Tom rushed to Bill and made a tourniquet to slow the bleeding. Then, Tom picked Bill up, put Bill on his back, and carried him over two miles through rough terrain to get to their car, all the while saying, "You hang in there, Bill. Don't you die on me. I'm going to get you to the hospital, and we are going to get you well."

Tom tenderly got Bill in the car and rushed him to a nearby hospital for emergency surgery. It went well, and afterward the doctor told Bill that he would be all right and that he would recover nicely. The doctor also told Bill what Bill already knew, that Tom had saved his life!

Some years later, Tom had to undergo heart surgery. Bill stayed with Tom and Tom's wife around the clock for days and days. He would not leave the hospital. He would not leave his best friend. The medical staff at the hospital noticed this. They told Bill not to worry, that everything was going great for Tom. He was recovering beautifully. They told Bill that it was OK to leave and get some rest because he must be exhausted. Bill thanked them for their concern, and then he told them the story of how Tom had carried him on his back for over two miles to save his life years before. And then he said: "After what Tom did for me, there is nothing I would not do for him. If it weren't for Tom, I wouldn't be here today. I owe him everything. I owe him my life!"

That's how Zacchaeus felt about what Jesus did for him, and that is precisely how we as Christians gratefully feel because that is precisely what Jesus Christ has done for us. He has saved our lives, so there is nothing we would not do for him because he is the one who has given us a new relationship with God, a new regard for others, and a new reason for living. When you have those three things in your life, you are rich indeed in the things that count the most.

Some years ago, I was a pastor at a church in a college town. One of my favorite persons in the congregation was a wonderful older man. Most everyone in that community called him Mr. Joe.

Mr. Joe was a kind-spirited man who was always gracious, thoughtful, and considerate to everyone. He was a real Christian gentleman. He was what I would call a "sweet conservative." He loved life. He loved people. He loved the church. He loved the Bible. He loved his Sunday school class. He loved our nation. He loved our president, whoever the president was, and he prayed for his president and his pastor every single day. And he also loved his wife, Mrs. Betty.

Mr. Joe and Mrs. Betty had been married for nearly sixty years when, one night, she died in her sleep. Mr. Joe was devastated. He and Mrs. Betty had been childhood sweethearts, and they had been an inspiration to everyone who knew them by the way they had loved and cared for each other over the years.

At Mrs. Betty's funeral, the church was packed. I was not surprised by that, but I was surprised to see Charles there.

Charles was also a member of our church, and he was the most liberal college professor in town. I had no idea that he and Mr. Joe were friends. Their approach to life was so different. They both were devoted Christians, but socially, politically, religiously, they were at the opposite ends of the pole. One was old, and one was young; one a conservative, the other a liberal; one a lifelong Republican, the other a lifelong Democrat.

And yet, here was Charles at the funeral. And on top of that, Charles was the lead pallbearer. In addition, as the memorial service began, Charles went over and sat beside Mr. Joe. Charles put his arm around Mr. Joe's shoulders and held him and patted him and comforted him throughout the service.

I was touched to see this, but I was mystified. I had no idea they were close friends—an unlikely pair, this older conservative man and this young, brilliant, fiercely liberal professor.

After the service, I mentioned to Mr. Joe that I didn't realize that he and Charles were friends. "Oh," he said. "We are next-door neighbors, have been for years, and we take care of each other. Charles is a terrific neighbor and a dear and wonderful friend. We have had coffee together every Wednesday morning for the last ten years. We see so many things differently. We laugh about it. I tell him that he cancels out all of my political votes, but I love Charles. He is like a son to me."

I asked Charles about their friendship, and he said, "I love Mr. Joe so much. We had an instant friendship when we first met. He is a great man. When my sister died in a tragic accident recently, Mr. Joe sat up with me all night. I've told him that he is like a father to me, and there is nothing I wouldn't do for him . . . except vote the way he does!"

Isn't that beautiful? Two men so different and yet united in the Christian spirit of caring.

It's beautiful to be extravagant in our compassion and in our caring.

There is an old story of two monks who are on their way back to their monastery when they are caught in a violent snowstorm. Struggling to make it back, they come across a man who has fallen and injured himself and is almost frozen to death. One of the monks tells the other that they must help get this man to the monastery or he will die in the elements. The other monk says that they cannot make it carrying the injured man and that they will all die. But the first insists that he will help the man, while the other decides to go on and save himself. The monk who stayed behind to help struggled and carried the man through the storm. Just before reaching the monastery, he tripped over a frozen body. It was the body of the monk who went on to save himself. The weather had overcome him, but the monk who helped the frozen man made it because his struggles and labor of carrying another had kept him from freezing. Jesus said, "Those who love their life lose it, and those who hate their life in this world will keep it for eternal life" (John 12:25).

Jesus was right, wasn't he? This is the way life works. We experience life best when we have a healthy relationship with God and a healthy regard for other people.

⚞ ⚞ ⚞ ⚞ ⚞

A businessman checked into a hotel late one night. He decided that he would stop in the lounge for a few minutes before going up to his room. Later that night, he called the front desk and asked, "What time will the lounge be opened in the morning?" The night clerk answered, "9:00 A.M." About an hour later, the man called again with the same question: "What time will the lounge be opened in the morning?" Again the clerk said, "9:00 A.M." The man called a third time, and a fourth, and every hour throughout the night. Each time the night clerk would answer: "9:00 A.M."

At 7:00 A.M. the hotel manager arrived, and the night clerk reported that everything had gone all right, except for this crazy man who kept calling the desk every hour asking what time the lounge would open. Just then the phone rang again. This time, the manager took the call. Sure enough, it was the same businessman, calling again with the same question about what time the lounge would open. The manager said, "Look here! The night clerk tells me that you have been a nuisance all night long, asking the same question. I am telling you for the last time, the lounge will be open at 9:00 A.M. You can't get in till then." To which the businessman replied, "Get *in*? I don't want to get *in*, I want to get *out*!"

In our world today, a lot of people feel trapped like that, and sadly they think that all they can do is just sit there. Psychologists tell us that as long as we live, there are two kinds of desires working within us, battling for our allegiance. One is the desire to give up and quit on life, to throw in the towel and congeal into some final self. The other is the desire to keep on moving forward, to keep on striving, to keep on learning, to keep on growing. And this is the calling of every Christian. This is the desire that keeps us young in spirit and beautifully alive. We must be constantly on guard against congealing. Or in other words, "You can't just sit there!"

CHAPTER THREE

STORIES OF PURPOSE AND MISSION

I have a friend I wish I could introduce to you. His name is Bret. At twenty years of age, if Bret were standing here beside me, he would not come up to my waist. I'll never forget the first time I saw him. He was eight years old, a third-grader at his elementary school. He was running in some races during the school's Field Day. I was so impressed by Bret's spunk and spirit. His competitors were so much larger than he was, so he didn't have much of a chance to win. I saw him run in three races that day, and in every one of them he finished last. But his mother stood at the finish line and waited for him. She would run and hug him and say, "Bret, you did real well, and I'm so proud of you!"

By the end of the day Bret had not won a single ribbon. But if I had had some Olympic gold medals, I would have put one on Bret, and one on his mother. Bret won the heart of everyone there, because he did his very best. He tried his hardest, he used what he had, and he gave his all.

Now, on that same day, there was another little boy the same age as Bret, sitting under a tree pouting, because he remembered that the year before he didn't win a blue ribbon. So this year he decided that rather than run and risk not winning first prize, he just wouldn't run at all. Rather than risk failure, he wouldn't try at all. The teachers were pleading with him to try, his mother was pleading with him to try, the other students were pleading with him to try, but he just sat there all day and pouted, and never got in the game at all.

Bret didn't win a blue ribbon, but he was a winner that day, and he still is. He's in college, drives a car, has a job, and smiles at everybody he meets. And everybody he meets loves him, because he uses what he has.

In the Olympics when the athletes take the awards stand and receive their medals, they are filled with joy and pride over what they have worked for and accomplished as the greatest athletes in the world but, let me ask you something, have you ever seen the Special Olympics, athletes with disabilities, of all ages, running and jumping and competing for all they are worth? Talk about joy and pride and accomplishment; look at the faces of those athletes. No joy could be greater, no pride could be greater because they are using their talents, challenged as they may be, to the fullest: and that's all God expects from any of his children.

G. A. Studdert-Kennedy once wrote a powerful and poignant poem that reminds us that it is the day in, day out commitment to God that really counts. He laments that sometimes we wish we could do one great deed and let that take care of everything, but the reality is that life doesn't work that way. This is not God's way or God's will. Rather, it is the way of daily discipleship. He puts it like this: We don't reach up to God by one grand or spectacular action, but instead it is "deed by deed and tear by tear, / Our souls must climb to thee."

Studdert-Kennedy only stated poetically what biblical writers declared long before, namely, if we can only serve in the small jobs, or in the remote corners or in the nitty-gritty areas, that's greatness in God's eyes—when we give our all. And there is joy and peace to be found even in those unlikely places of menial service. It's not what you have, but how you use what you have that brings peace and joy and fulfillment. God expects us to be the best we can be and to use our talents to the fullest. It's not how big your position is, it's not how big your talent is, it's only how big your heart is that matters.

There is a true story that comes from the sinking of the *Titanic*. A frightened woman found her place in a lifeboat that was about to be lowered into the frigid waters of the North Atlantic on that tragic April night of 1912. The woman suddenly thought of something she needed, so she asked permission to return to her stateroom before they cast off. She was told that she could have only three minutes, otherwise, they would have to leave without her; and she could only bring back one thing.

The woman ran across the deck which was already slanted at a dangerous angle. She hurried through the room where people had been taking bets. Everywhere she looked, she could see money floating in the ankle-deep water. She ignored it and rushed on to her room. There she reached for her jewelry box, which contained her diamond rings and her expensive bracelets, her necklaces and other priceless jewelry. But then suddenly, her eyes fell on another box—a box that contained a few apples and three small oranges. She could only take one box back to the lifeboat, and the clock was ticking. Which one should she choose? What would you have done? Which one would you have chosen? The jewels or the fresh fruit? The crown or the cross? The priceless gems or the food to save lives in a lifeboat?

The woman quickly made her choice. She pushed the jewel box aside, grabbed the box with the apples and oranges, and ran back to the lifeboat and got in.

Fascinating, isn't it? Thirty minutes before, that woman would never have chosen a box of fruit over even the smallest diamond. But that life situation suddenly changed her perspective and gave her a new way of looking at things, a new way of measuring value, a new way of deciding what is important.

When we in faith accept Jesus Christ into our lives as Lord and Savior, he changes our perspective like that. He gives us a new vision, a new wisdom, a new stance, new priorities, a new way of deciding what is really valuable. He shows us how to choose the cross of service over the crown of riches.

Ingratitude leads to apathy, and apathy is the worst failure of all.

J. Wallace Hamilton, in his book *Ride the Wild Horses*, tells a wonderful story about how easy it is to take for granted what we have. It's about a farmer who had lived on the same farm all his life and was tired of it, bored with it. He had inherited the farm from his father, but now he desperately craved a change. He subjected everything on the farm to his own blind and merciless criticism.

At last, he decided that he would sell the old place and buy another more to his liking. So he listed the farm with a real-estate agent, who at once came out and looked over the property, and the two men prepared a sales advertisement for the newspaper. Before giving the ad to the newspaper, however, the agent read to the farmer the ad's very flattering description of the farm: "Beautiful farmhouse, ideal location, excellent barn, good pasture, fertile soil, up-to-date equipment, well-bred stock. Near town, near church, near school. Good neighbors."

"Wait a minute," said the farmer. "Read that over again, and take it slow." Again the description was read: "Beautiful farmhouse, ideal location," and so forth.

"Changed my mind," said the farmer. "I'm not gonna sell. All my life I've been looking for a place just like that!"

Can't we relate to that? That farmer was living in a paradise, and he didn't know it.

At Barbara Bush's literacy conference here in Houston in the spring of 2002, one of the featured authors was Ronan Tynan. You may recognize that name. He is one of the world-famous Irish tenors. In addition to commenting on his book, Dr. Tynan was coaxed back onstage to sing "Danny Boy," and then with everyone standing, he sang "God Bless America." It was magnificent.

In his book *Halfway Home: My Life 'til Now*, Ronan Tynan shares his remarkable story of overcoming adversity and attaining worldwide success in several different areas. He is an award-winning singer, an award-winning athlete, an award-winning horseman, an award-winning doctor, and an award-winning writer. His accomplishments are even more amazing when you realize that he was born with a serious lower-limb disability, causing him to spend the first three years of his life in the hospital and to have his legs amputated when he was twenty years old.

How did Ronan Tynan do it? How was he able to accomplish so much while standing, walking, and running on prosthetic legs? He credits his friends, his teachers, his family, and his faith, but especially his father, who encouraged him and supported him and affirmed him and loved him day-in and day-out. Ronan Tynan said that the teasing and narrow-minded comments of some people did get to him, but they didn't stay with him, because he always remembered his father. That's what kept him going—the love and affirmation and encouragement of his father.

Over the years, scholars have debated what is the most intense desire within human beings. Some have said it is the will to pleasure; others have said it is the will to power; others have said it is the will to happiness; still others have said it is the will to security. Viktor Frankl, coming out of the prison camp in World War II, said he believed it was the will to meaning; and I believe he's right. Nothing is more important than having a sense of meaning in what you do.

This idea is one I see often in people's kitchens, usually on some piece of art hanging over the sink. It's a prayer-poem that celebrates the sacredness of practical work like preparing meals and washing dishes. In essence the prayer admits to God that most of us will never be famous saints, but we can bring love and warmth and joy to our work in the kitchen with the pots and pans, and that all work that is dedicated to God is indeed sacred. The prayer-poem then ends with these words: "Accept this service that I do, I do it unto Thee."

"I do it unto Thee"—this is indeed the key to meaning in our lives, to do everything we do as if God were our employer, to do everything we do as if we were doing it for God as his partner, as his coworker.

What does God expect of us? The parable of the talents makes it clear: God expects us to be the best we can be. He expects us to use our talents to the fullest, and he expects us to make our work meaningful and productive and creative by seeing our work as unto the Lord.

People with a purpose are never lazy. Their work becomes an exciting expression of their faith and cause. A good case in point is Mother Teresa.

Mother Teresa worked for many years with a leper colony called the Home for the Destitute and Dying. Her work was zestful and vibrant because she saw Christ in it so vividly.

She pretended that every person she met was Christ in disguise! Why don't you try that sometime? It will change your life.

Here is Mother Teresa's daily prayer. She called it "Jesus, My Patient."

> Dearest Lord, may I see you today and every day in the person of your sick, and, whilst nursing them, minister unto you. Though you hide yourself behind the unattractive disguise of the irritable, the exacting, the unreasonable, may I still recognize you, and say: "Jesus, my patient, how sweet it is to serve you." Lord, give me this seeing faith, then my work will never be monotonous. I will ever find joy in humoring the fancies and gratifying the wishes of all poor sufferers. O beloved sick, how doubly dear you are to me, when you personify Christ, and what a privilege is mine to be allowed to tend you.

How is it with you? Do you have that kind of purpose in your work? Or are you like the one-talent servant: locked in a prison of boredom and laziness and emptiness?

⟞⟝ ⟞⟝ ⟞⟝ ⟞⟝ ⟞⟝

Phillip Childs, a pastor with Parakletos Ministries in Decatur, Georgia, tells an intriguing story about a class of fourth graders in a public elementary school. The children were hard at work. The ten-year-old students were furiously writing, filling their pages with a list of "I Can'ts": "I can't kick the soccer ball past second base." "I can't do long division with more than three numbers." "I can't get Debbie to like me." Their pages were full, and they showed no signs of letting up.

Every student was writing his or her "I Can't" list. The teacher was also doing the same: "I can't get John's mother to come for a teacher conference." "I can't get my daughter to put gas in the car." "I can't get Alan to use words rather than fists." Why were they dwelling on the negative instead of writing the more positive "I Can" statements? Soon, the answer came.

The teacher stood up and said, "Okay, children, let's do it!" The children ran forward and put all of their "I Can't" lists into a shoe box. The teacher then grabbed a shovel and the shoe box and marched outside. The students followed close behind. They walked to the farthest corner of the school yard, and, one by one, they all took turns with the shovel. They were digging a grave!

When the grave was ready, thirty-one ten-year-olds stood there as their teacher placed the shoe box at the bottom of the hole. They covered it with dirt, and then the teacher said, "Boys and girls, please join hands and bow your heads." They did, and the teacher gave the eulogy.

> Friends, we are gathered here today to honor the memory of "I Can't." While he was here with us on earth he touched the lives of everyone, some more than others. We have provided "I Can't" with a final resting place and a headstone that contains his epitaph. He is survived by his brothers and sisters, "I Can," "I Will," and "I'm Going to Right Away." They are not as well known as their famous relative and are certainly not as strong and powerful yet. Perhaps some day, with your help, they will make an even bigger mark on the world. May "I Can't" rest in peace and may everyone present pick up their lives and move forward in his absence. Amen. (Phillip B. Childs, "The I Can't Funeral," *North Texas United Methodist Reporter* 31 [January 22, 1999]: 1)

What a great moment this was. These students would never forget this. But they weren't through yet. The group went back to the classroom and had cookies and popcorn and fruit juice. The teacher cut a large tombstone from brown paper. She wrote the words "I Can't" at the top and "Rest in Peace" at the bottom, and then she wrote the date. She hung the tombstone on the bulletin board for the rest of the year, and on those rare occasions when a student would feel defeated and say "I can't," the teacher would simply point to the "Rest in Peace" sign. The student would then remember that "I Can't" was dead and buried, and he or she would then resolve to try harder.

Jesus would like this story, I believe, because that is what he was saying to those first disciples: "You can do it. I will help you. Don't just sit there in defeat. Come on now. Get up and follow me." The apostle Paul would probably like this story too, because one of his most famous quotes says it all: "I can do all things through [Christ] who strengthens me" (Philippians 4:13).

The point is clear: The choice is ours. We can wallow in defeat, feel sorry for ourselves, and say, "We can't do anything about the complex problems that surround us"; or we can hear the call of Jesus and respond with courage and optimism and faith. To those early disciples long ago, and to you and me here and now, Jesus is saying, "Don't just sit there in defeat! Get up and come and follow me! You can *do* it. I will help you."

She was a delightful woman and very well advanced in years. She had purchased a small booklet the day before for twenty-five cents, and she liked it so much that she came back to buy another one for a friend of hers. As the clerk fixed her package, the woman noticed that the price of the booklet was now thirty-five cents. "But I only paid *a quarter* yesterday," she remarked. "No, ma'am," the clerk answered, "the price has been the same all week—thirty-five cents. I mark the books myself."

So the woman dug the rest of the cost from the bottom of her purse, saying, "Sorry I was such a bother," and she turned to leave.

The man behind her stepped up to the cash register, but then the woman turned back, stepped in front of him, and said, "I'm terribly sorry to interrupt, but there's one more thing I need to take care of with this young woman." The woman laid her handbag down on the counter and began to search it as best she could. "I hate to be such a bother but this is important," she said, as she smiled back at the growing line of people at the cash register.

The search continued but with no luck. Finally she put down her shawl and her packages and got both hands in her purse and searched and searched. Then, she found what she had been looking for, and out from the bottom of her handbag was lifted a single coin—a dime. Handing it to the clerk, she said, "This is for yesterday. I only paid you twenty-five cents for my booklet yesterday, so I owe you another dime."

"Oh, no, that's all right," the clerk said, trying to refuse the dime.

But the woman was insistent. "Oh, you must accept it. It's the only honest thing to do."

A big, gruff-looking man standing in line with a cigar in his mouth spoke up: "You're right, little lady. It always pays to be honest."

"Oh, no," the woman answered, stuffing the other items back into her purse. "No, it *costs* to be honest. It just cost me a dime; but Jesus is honest, and I try my best to be like him."

There was a glint from a tear in the eye of the clerk as she rang up the cash register.

Ten cents; one thin dime. Ten cents. Too many of us lose our standards or water down our commitments when life is just ordinary. Too many of us, too often, just drift in the stream. The writer of Hebrews tells us not to be like that. He tells us not to throw away what we know is right but rather to endure and do the will of God.

Honesty costs. Discipleship costs. Christianity costs in ordinary day-to-day living because it means what that woman knew. It means "being like Jesus," and trying to be like Jesus is what makes the most ordinary times extraordinary. So it is important—vitally important—to seize the day and live faithfully now.

◄━━ ◄━━ ◄━━ ◄━━ ◄━━

It had been some time since Jack had seen the wonderful older man who lived next door. Through the years, college, dating, career, the rush to success, and life itself had all gotten in the way. In the hectic pace of his busy life, Jack had had little time to think about the past, and now, often no time to spend with his wife and son. He was working on the future, and nothing could stop him.

But then came the phone call. It was his mother, and she said, "Mr. Belser died last night. The funeral is Wednesday." Memories flashed through Jack's mind like an old newsreel, as he sat quietly remembering his childhood days.

"Jack, did you hear me?"

"Oh, sorry, Mom. Yes, I heard you. It's been so long since I thought of him. I'm sorry, but I honestly thought he died years ago," Jack said.

"Well, he didn't forget you, Jack. Every time I saw him, he'd ask how you were doing. He'd reminisce about the many days you spent over on 'his side of the fence,' as he put it," his mother told him.

"I loved that old house he lived in," Jack said.

"You know, Jack, after your father died, Mr. Belser stepped in to make sure you had a man's influence in your life," his mother said.

"I know," Jack said. "He's the one who taught me carpentry. I wouldn't be in this business if it weren't for him. He spent a lot of time teaching me things he thought were important. Mom, I'll be there for the funeral."

As busy as he was, Jack kept his word. He caught the next flight to his hometown. Mr. Belser's funeral was small and brief. He had no children of his own, and most of his relatives had passed away.

The night before he had to return home, Jack and his mother stopped by to see the old house next door one more time. Standing in the doorway, Jack paused for a moment. It was like going back in time. The house was exactly as he remembered it. Every step, every picture, and every piece of furniture held warm and wonderful memories. But suddenly, Jack stopped.

"What's wrong, Jack?" his mother asked.

"The box is gone," Jack said.

"What box?"

"There was a small gold box that he kept locked on top of his desk. I must have asked him a thousand times what was in the box, and Mr. Belser would always say, 'Jack, in that box is the thing I value most these days,' but he never told me what it was." But now the box was gone. Jack and his mother decided that a member of the Belser family had taken it, and that they would never know what it was that was so valuable to Mr. Belser.

Jack flew back home and went back to work the next day. A day or so later, a package arrived in the mail for Jack. The return address caught Jack's immediate attention: It was Mr. Belser's name and address.

Jack ripped into the package. Inside was the gold box. His heart racing, Jack carefully opened the gold box, and inside he found a beautiful gold pocket-watch. Cautiously, he unlatched the cover. Inside, he found engraved on the watch cover these words: *Jack, thanks for your time! Harold Belser.*

Jack swallowed hard as he realized: Oh my goodness, the thing Mr. Belser valued most was my time. Jack held the watch in his hand thoughtfully for just a few minutes. Then he called his office and cleared his appointments for the next two days. "Why?" his assistant Janet asked. "Because," Jack said, "I need to spend some time with my wife and my son. And oh, by the way, Janet—thanks for your time!"

I like that story because it reminds us of a very important truth of life that we are so prone to forgetting in this busy, hectic, pressure-packed, competitive, success-oriented world in which we live, namely this: Life is not measured by the number of things we accumulate or the number of awards we win or the number of successes we achieve or the number of honors we receive or the wealth we pile up or the number of years we put in. No, in the final analysis, the bottom line is this: It's not the number of breaths we take, it's the number of moments that take our breath away.

Leo Buscaglia told a wonderful story about a student he had at the University of Southern California (USC) some years ago. The student's name was Joel, and Joel was absolutely miserable. Joel felt useless and worthless and joyless. He was depressed. One day Joel told his professor, Buscaglia, how unhappy and how unfulfilled he was. In despair, Joel said, "There is not one thing in my life that is worthwhile." Buscaglia said, "Okay Joel, let's go make a visit." Buscaglia took Joel over to the convalescent hospital near the campus at USC. Inside there were many older people, lying on beds, staring at the ceiling. As they walked into that scene, Joel looked around and said, "What am I doing here? I don't know anything about gerontology." Buscaglia said, "Good. You see that lady over there on the bed? Go over and say hello to her."

"That's all?" Joel asked.

"Yes, just go over there and say hello."

So Joel went over to the woman and said hello. She looked at him suspiciously and asked, "Are you a relative?" Joel said, "No." And she said, "Good. Sit down."

So Joel sat down and they started to talk. Buscaglia wrote: "My goodness, the things she told him. She told him all kinds of things about love, about pain, about suffering, and even about approaching death and dying...with which she had made her own peace. She knew all these things, but nobody cared to listen to her" (except now Joel).

Well, Joel started going to visit once a week. It was so regular that in the hospital they named that day "Joel's Day." Buscaglia said that the greatest day in his teaching career was when he was walking across the campus one Saturday afternoon, and there was Joel, like a pied piper, with thirty older people stretched out behind him. He was taking them to the coliseum to see a football game.

Somewhere in heaven God was smiling because that's God's way—to find your life, your joy, your meaning, and your mission by reaching out in love to help other people.

Jesus put it like this: "Whoever will lose himself will find himself." The key to life is to seek God's will, to obey God's word, and to live God's way to make God the number one priority in your life!

There is an old legend that emphasizes an important point. The story tells of Jesus' return to heaven after his time on earth and the angels gather to hear his account of what happened there on earth. Jesus tells them about his miracles and his teachings and then tells of the pain of his arrest, trial, and crucifixion, and of the glory of resurrection. When Jesus finished his account, one of the angels asks Jesus, "But what happens now?" Jesus said: "I have left behind eleven faithful disciples and a handful of men and women who have faithfully followed me. They will declare my message, express my love, and build my church. They will share and witness to the faith to their friends, and they will share with theirs until the whole world will know their story and the gospel." But the angel said, "What if they fail? Or, what if at some point in history the people of the church fail or cease their witness? What is the alternative plan?" Jesus answered: "I have no other plan. I am depending upon them." The gift of the Spirit is the gift of purpose and mission.

Some folks in the church act as if they have a first-class ticket. They just sit there, and they expect to be catered to and waited on. "Let someone else do the dirty work! Not me!" is their cry.

The largest McDonald's restaurant in the world opened some years ago in Moscow, the capital city of Russia. It seats more than seven hundred people. Projections were that this one restaurant would bring in approximately fifteen million dollars a year, and it is doing that. The Russian people are rushing to McDonald's for a "Bolshoi Mac."

Now, it's interesting to me that many of the Russian people who have dined under the golden arches in Moscow say that it's not the Western food that impresses them so much, but it's the way the employees cater to them.

"May I help you?"

"What can I do for you?"

"What would you like?"

"May I serve you?"

"Please enjoy your meal!"

"Have a nice afternoon."

"You deserve a break today," all said with a lilt in the voice and a warm, caring smile.

The Russian people were not used to that. But most of us are! We expect to be pampered when we go to a restaurant, and if we are not treated with excellent service, we are very disappointed. It's part of what we call our "cater culture," and that's fine. We all enjoy that.

However, we have to be careful not to let that "cater culture" mind-set cloud our understanding of the real purpose of the church. We join the church to become not God's privileged people, but God's servant people; not God's pampered people, but God's workforce.

Recently, the Holocaust Museum in Houston had an elegant luncheon to present their "Guardian of the Human Spirit" awards. Awards were presented to the *Houston Chronicle* and to one of our church members, Jack Blanton. June and I get to go to a lot of nice events in Houston and in the state of Texas because of Jack, who is often and appropriately recognized and honored for his great leadership in our city and state.

Because Jack was one of the honorees, I was asked to come and be on the program. Jack always takes care of us and sees to it that we get to sit with his family. There were twelve people standing around our table, and we recognized everybody there except one couple. "Who is that man?" I asked somebody, and the answer came back, "That's Luci's husband." I wanted to say, "Luci *who?*" but thankfully, I didn't.

Later, as we were being seated, someone said, "Just sit anywhere you would like, but Luci's purse is in this chair, so we will let her sit here, and everybody else, just find a place." I wondered, *Who in the world is Luci?* Moments later, I found out. The event hosts recognized a long list of honored guests—someone from the governor's office, the mayor pro tem, senators and legislators, members of the city council, survivors of the Holocaust. And then finally, the master of ceremonies said, "And of course, we are delighted to have with us today Luci Baines Johnson"— daughter of the late U.S. President Lyndon Baines Johnson"— and with that, the Luci at our table stood up! And I thought, *Oh, that Luci!*

She was delightful! She asked about our church and told me that she had visited it several times for weddings, funerals, and once for Sunday worship, and she said, "It is always such an exciting experience to be in St. Luke's." I loved that!

I asked about her mother, the former First Lady, Lady Bird Johnson. Mrs. Johnson had had a stroke the previous spring, but Luci said that she was doing better. In those first days after the stroke, Mrs. Johnson could not communicate, but she later improved to the point that she could, with effort, communicate with her family. Luci said to me, "I want to tell you an amazing story." She said when her mother had her stroke, she sat beside her bed each day, held her hand, and said, "Mother, I'm going to pray the Lord's Prayer...." She prayed. No response from Mrs. Johnson.

Luci did that again every day for several days. Still no response.

On the Saturday before Pentecost Sunday she did it again, and this time Mrs. Johnson tried to join in. She moved her lips but no words came out. On Sunday, Pentecost Sunday (the birthday of the church, the celebration of God's gift of the Holy Spirit), when Luci held her mother's hand and began to pray the Lord's Prayer, Luci said, "Our Father..." and clear as a bell, Mrs. Johnson said, "Who art in heaven." Later that day, Luci told the doctor what had happened and asked how her mother was able to do that. And the doctor replied, "Because she has been saying those words for eighty-four years!"

Mrs. Johnson had her own personal commitment to Christ for all those years, her own ark of spiritual strength. And now, when crisis had come, she had the grace and strength that came from years of practicing her faith.

And the Lord said, "Go!"
And I said, "Who, me?"
And he said, "Yes, you."
And I said, "But, Lord, I'm not ready yet. I'm not prepared yet. I'm not psyched up yet. Besides I'm needed here."
And God said, "You're stalling." Again, the Lord said, "Go!"
And I said, "But I don't want to."
And he said, "I didn't ask if you wanted to."
And I said, "Listen, Lord. I'm not that kind of person. I'm not talented enough to represent you. I'm not good enough. I don't want to get into controversy. Besides, my family may not like this. And what will the neighbors say?"
And God said, "You're stalling again."
And yet a third time, the Lord said, "Go!"
And I said "Do I have to?"
And he said, "Do you love me?"
And I said, "Lord, you know I love you. But look—I'm scared.

People are going to ridicule me and cut me into little pieces. And I just can't take that all by myself."

And God said, "Where do you think I'll be?" Again the Lord said, "Go! And I will go with you!"

And I prayed, "Here am I, Lord. Send me."

Some years ago, I was driving home from work when I saw something that touched me deeply. It had just started raining and people were scurrying about trying to escape the rain, and then I saw it. A young mother was out in her front yard with her two-year-old daughter, and they were celebrating the rain, enjoying the rain, relishing the rain, savoring the rain. Like Gene Kelly in the classic movie, they were "singing in the rain!" With arms out-stretched, faces lifted toward the heavens, they were welcoming the rain. They were getting drenched, but they were giggling with delight, enjoying every moment of it and singing loudly the doxology:

> Praise God, from whom all blessings flow;
> Praise him, all creatures here below;
> Praise him above, ye heavenly host;
> Praise Father, Son, and Holy Ghost.
> (Thomas Ken, 1674)

Isn't that beautiful? While others were trying to escape the rain, seeing it as a problem or an inconvenience, that young mother was teaching her daughter how to celebrate the soft rain as a blessing from God.

The point is clear: With all the stresses and problems in this life, still the truth is we have so many doxologies to sing, so much to be grateful for, and so many blessings to count. The point is, life is more than a grueling endurance test. Life is more than a survival game. Life is more than a coping competition.

So you see, it's not enough just to escape the stress. It's not enough just to endure the stress. Thank God, there is another option.

———— ———— ———— ———— ————

Sometimes we experience breathtaking moments in our life which are so powerful that words cannot describe them; we can only exclaim, "Ah!" in admiration. The high moments of "Ah!" are available to all of us. They are as near as breathing, all around us—if only we could open our eyes to see them, our ears to hear them, and our hands to touch them.

Many of these "ah" moments are very ordinary, day-to-day things. Recently I ran across a list of breathtaking "ah" moments that can be triggered by some very ordinary, everyday experiences:

- The celebration of God's incredible creation, the seashore or the mountains, a beautiful sunrise or sunset
- A tender love experience—that very special moment in life when you and another person become as one and, if only for a moment, become the whole world for each other
- Childbirth—especially the sight of the first child (or grandchild)
- Physical exercise, such as walking or swimming and, for some people, running, and for others, gardening
- A religious experience—feeling the presence of God powerfully in your life
- Art—especially religious art
- Scientific or intellectual discovery, such as solving a difficult math problem
- Poetry or soul-stirring music
- Creative work
- Recollection and reflection
- Beauty—encountering the beautiful

How did you do? Anything there that makes you exclaim,

"Ah"? All of them touched me, with the possible exception of the math problem. Solving a math problem makes me say, "Whew!" rather than "Ah!"

In the Scriptures, we see that those who have the "ah" experiences are equipped to better handle the blahs when they come. Remember Moses at the burning bush? That was a breathtaking "ah" moment, and it served him well later when he surely must have faced the blahs as he tried to deal with a dangerous pharaoh and a difficult people.

Or what about Jacob? Remember how he cheated and connived; but then, in a dream, he saw a ladder leading to heaven. He encountered God, an "ah" experience, and he expressed it for all of us: "Surely the LORD is in this place—and I did not know it!" (Genesis 28:12, 16). I wonder how many times God has been in the place where we were and we didn't know it; we missed it; we didn't understand or perceive it. If it could happen to a renegade like Jacob, it could happen to us.

Our need is not so much to create the breathtaking "ah" experiences and situations, but to celebrate the ones that are all around us. This calls for sensitivity and openness that some of us may not have at this moment. One thing is for sure: We all need the eyes of faith! How easy it is to miss our high moment because we don't expect it, because we are blind to it or refuse to open our eyes. "God is in this place"—and we need to learn how to see him and feel him and know the "Ah!" of his presence. Nothing will help us handle the blahs better than that.

———

This is a true story, but one that may make you say, "Only in California." Larry Walters was a thirty-something truck driver who lived in Los Angeles. He lived in one of those neighborhoods where all of the houses looked alike, and where each of the yards was surrounded by a chain-link fence. Every Saturday afternoon, Larry had a ritual. He would sit in a lawn chair, sip a cool beverage, and just relax for a couple of hours. This is what he would do every Saturday afternoon in his backyard.

One Saturday, however, Larry got a bright idea. He decided that he would tie some helium balloons to his lawn chair, enough to float himself about one hundred feet or so over his neighbors' yards. It should be noted at this point that Larry was not an aeronautics engineer. Therefore, he didn't *really* know how many helium balloons it would take to elevate him to the desired height of one hundred feet.

So Larry purchased forty-five weather balloons and filled them with helium. Then he packed some sandwiches, prepared his cool beverage, and took along a BB gun so that he could shoot out one or more of the balloons if he got too high. Next, with the help of his neighbors, he tied the balloons to his lawn chair. (Let me digress just long enough to say: "Don't try this at home!")

At the appropriate signal, the neighbors let go of the ropes that tethered the "balloon-chair." Larry immediately rocketed up to 11,000 feet! No kidding! He was so shocked and so frightened that he never got a chance to shoot any of the balloons out with his BB gun; instead, he was too busy holding on to the lawn chair. Larry was first spotted by a DC-10 pilot flying into Los Angeles International Airport; he had zipped up into one of the busiest flight patterns in the world. The DC-10 pilot radioed the tower that there was a man on a lawn chair at 11,000 feet, and that he had a gun! Planes were immediately rerouted around the spot where Larry was floating. Rescue craft were sent up, and eventually they got Larry safely back down to the ground with his lawn chair. He was, of course, quickly surrounded by reporters who had rushed out to get the story on this bizarre (even for California) event. Reporters asked Larry, "Were you scared?"

"No," Larry said.

"Would you do it again?"

"No."

"Well, why did you do it in the first place?"

Larry replied, "Well—you can't just *sit* there!"

Now, strange as it may seem, when I first heard the story of Larry's big adventure that Saturday afternoon in Los Angeles, it made me think of the first chapter of Mark, where Jesus came to Simon, Andrew, James, and John at the seashore and called them to be his disciples. In effect, Jesus said to them: Don't just sit there doing the same old things, performing the same old rituals, living the same old life. Break out of the drudgery! Do something good—exciting—come and follow me!

Please don't misunderstand me. I am not applauding Larry and his lawn chair and helium balloons. Obviously, that was a dangerous and crazy thing to do. He could have been killed. He could have caused all kinds of problems, and in fact, he did. He could have hurt someone else. Indeed, his exploits that day could have produced a major calamity. But even though he went about it the wrong way, what is significant to notice here is this: There was something stirring deep down inside of Larry, telling him that just sitting there was not enough. There is more to life than just sitting there.

CHAPTER FOUR

STORIES OF HURT
AND HEALING

Have you ever wondered why people in the United States are so crazy about football? I think I figured that out some years ago at a high-school football game. There in a short period of two hours, the full spectrum of human emotions was played out. In that brief period of time, those of us who were there as interested and involved spectators experienced the gamut of feelings—joy and sorrow, agony and ecstasy, chills and thrills, ups and downs, "ahs" and "blahs." The team I was rooting for fell behind 13-0, and everybody on our side of the stadium felt so sad, so blue, so blah.

But then in the fourth quarter, our team rallied and scored two touchdowns and went ahead 14-13, with less than two minutes left in the game. We were deliriously happy. People were hugging and jumping and shouting and crying tears of joy. Our band was playing loudly, the cheerleaders were cheering, the pep squad was waving their pompoms, and the players were celebrating on the sideline with magnificent high-fives. It was an "ah" moment, a moment to relish, a moment to savor.

But four plays later, the other team completed a fifty-seven-yard pass play for a touchdown, and then they had the "ahs" and we had the "blahs." We sat in stunned, stony, sad silence as the final seconds ticked off the clock. So quickly our ecstasy had turned to agony; so quickly our victory had turned to defeat; so quickly our joy had turned to sorrow. I kept saying to myself, *It's just a ballgame*, and it was; and yet, in a way, it was something more—it was a microcosm of life. It was a strange and wonderful and confusing mix of some of our most powerful emotions.

Through that experience, I realized again what I already knew, namely, that life for all of us is a dramatic mixture of moods and feelings and happenings. Life is no smooth railroad trip across level plains; but rather it is more like a roller-coaster ride, with the "ahs" of the mountaintop and the "blahs" of the valley. We can all remember those high moments of joy when life feels good and really worth the living. However, we also know those low moments of depression and discouragement when we feel hope-less and we are ready to throw in the towel and give up on life. We have all experienced both the "ahs" and "blahs" of life. We can all relate to the words of the spiritual: "Sometimes I'm up, sometimes I'm down, oh, yes, Lord."

⟞⟝ ⟞⟝ ⟞⟝ ⟞⟝ ⟞⟝

I believe with all my heart that the way to a lasting peace resides in Jesus Christ—in what he came for and stood for and died for; in his intense pursuit of truth, love, and justice. That is precisely what this story in Mark 5 is all about. Christ walks into the tormented life of the Gerasene demoniac, this madman, who is at war with everybody and whose life is coming apart at the seams, and Jesus turns it around for him. He gives him the heal-ing he needs, and brings peace to his troubled soul.

At the beginning of this narrative, it sounds like a horror story. This wild-eyed, adrenaline-filled madman comes running and shrieking out of the tombs. This is an eerie, grim, suspenseful sit-uation. Jesus and his disciples have just come through a storm on the Sea of Galilee. It is nighttime and having survived that frightening storm, they are thrilled to now set foot on solid ground. But as they get out of the boat, they encounter a different kind of storm, yet another scary experience. They hear strange sounds coming from the tombs: shrieks, growls, screams, moans, the rattling of chains. Then suddenly, a horrifying sight! A madman in tattered clothes, bruised, dirty, bloody, and battered, with pieces of chains dangling from his arms and ankles, comes running and screaming directly toward them.

Now, let me ask you something: what would you have done in that situation? This was a perilous place, a bloodcurdling moment, with a powerful, dangerous, berserk man charging Jesus and his disciples. I think I would have run for my life or jumped back in the boat. But not Jesus! Jesus stood his ground and faced the madman, undaunted and unafraid. Jesus stood there and dealt with this wild man. Jesus healed him. Jesus brought peace to his troubled soul. He changed him, cleansed him. Jesus turned his life around. And you know, don't you, that he can do that for you and me, and he can do that for our world.

Please notice something here. The madman said his name was Legion. That's a military word, and so appropriate in this case because this man was at war. He was at war with himself. He was at war with other people. He was at war with God. And Jesus, the Prince of Peace, healed him. Jesus, the Prince of Peace, gave him peace within, peace with others, and peace with God.

He can do that for you and me. And he can do that for our world, which today is so like Legion, so desperately in need of peace within, peace with others, and peace with God. Remember how he put it in John 16: "In the world you have tribulation. Be courageous, for I have overcome the world" (v. 33, author's translation).This means that Christ endured the worst this world can dish out and was victorious over it. This means that what he represented cannot be defeated. His truth cannot be killed; it resurrects! His love cannot be stopped; it endures! God cannot be defeated; ultimately he wins, and through faith in him, the Peace, the Healing, the Victory, the New Life can be ours. And this is why it is so crucial, so vital, with the help of God to make Jesus Christ the Prince of Peace the priority of your life.

David came out of seminary ready to solve all the problems of the world single-handedly. He had been trained, he had studied hard, he had been a good student, and now, as a pastor in a little community in Virginia, he was ready to lay religion on the people. He was ready to give his answers with a pious, religious, authoritative tone. David thought he had all the answers, thought he was in complete control, thought he was "the answer man," as the months passed quickly by.

One day the telephone rang in his study. The father of a board chairman of the church suddenly had died. As David started to the family's home, it suddenly hit him: *I don't know what to say. I'm their pastor, and I'm scared.* David tried to recall appropriate Scripture passages to quote. He tried to think of some theological message to give these people in their shocked hour of need. He plotted his strategy: "I'll go in, gather all the family in the living room, and quote the Twenty-third Psalm. That's what I'll do; that's the answer!" But there was something David hadn't counted on. When he got to the home and gathered the family in the living room, as he looked across those mournful faces, he realized for the first time how much he loved these people. His heart broke along with them; he was overcome with emotion. He loved these people, and their hurt was his hurt; and as he opened his mouth to say the Twenty-third Psalm, no words would come, only sobs. David burst into tears, and he cried his eyes out. So much so, that the family had to come over to minister to him. David was so embarrassed, so ashamed. He felt that he had failed his people in their hour of need.

Shortly after, David was transferred to another church. Fifteen years or so passed. One day, David ran into that board chairman. David winced as he remembered that day, but then something happened that surprised him. The man's face lit up, he ran to David and hugged him tightly, and he said, "Oh, David, I'm so glad to see you! Our family loves and appreciates you so much. We miss you! We talk about you all the time. We'll never forget the time when Daddy died, how you came and cried with us!" David couldn't give answers that day, but unknowingly he had given that family something better: he had given them his love. We need to beware of presuming that we have all the answers.

Forgiveness is a gift. It can't be earned; it can't be bought—it can only be given by the one who has been wronged. Let me show you what I mean.

A few years ago, I received a long-distance, collect call from Boston. I accepted the call because I recognized the name of the young man calling. His name was Brad. He was seventeen years old, a runaway. A year or so before, Brad had been left in charge of the family store, and that night (after a heated argument with his dad) he had emptied the cash register, robbed his own family, and run away. His family had not heard from him for more than a year.

On the phone that morning he said, "Jim, I want to come home! I'm so ashamed of what I have done to my family. I'm really sorry and I want to come back, but I don't know if my folks will forgive me, and I wouldn't blame them if they didn't. I know I don't deserve it, but I'd like to have another chance. Can you help me?" We agreed that I would talk to his parents and get their answer, and that Brad would call my office at four o'clock that afternoon for the verdict.

That afternoon at exactly four o'clock, the phone rang. When

I answered it, Brad didn't even take the time to identify himself, he was so anxious that he blurted out, "What did they say?" I said, "Just a minute, Brad. There's someone here who wants to speak to you," and I handed the phone to his father. I'll never forget what his father said: "Son, we want you to come home. We've looked everywhere for you. I'm so glad to hear your voice. I'm so glad you're safe. You know, of course, that you have hurt us deeply, our hearts have been broken, but we love you, and we forgive you. Your mother and I will be on the next plane to Boston. We are coming to get you and to bring you home."

That's how forgiveness happens—the only way it happens—as a free gift from the one who has been wronged. It can't be earned or bought. It's a gift. In this parable in Matthew 18, God is the gracious king who freely cancels our debt, who freely forgives, not because of our goodness but because of his goodness, mercy, and unconditional love.

When I was in my middle year of seminary at the Methodist Theological School in Ohio, I took a course called Pastoral Care. In addition to the academic study, they also assigned us to be interns in a nearby facility so we could get practical experience along with our classroom work. I was assigned to be the student chaplain on the eighth floor of the Riverside Methodist Hospital in Columbus, Ohio. That was really exciting, to be the chaplain for the neurosurgery ward.

Every Thursday at 1:00 P.M., I would show up on the eighth floor and check in with the head nurse, and she would tell me about the patients: "This one had surgery two days ago." "This one is going home tomorrow." And I would go visit them. I would write up what the professors called "verbatims" and take them back to show the professor what the patient had said and what I had said. The professor would always write, "You talked too much."

One Thursday afternoon at one o'clock, the elevator doors opened, and the head nurse was standing there waiting for me. She said, "Jim, we need you today. We've never needed a minister more than we need one today. Mrs. Davis in 858 is supposed to have brain surgery at 8:00 A.M. She may not even make it off the table. There is a 50 percent chance she won't even survive the surgery, she is so ill. And she has quit on us. She won't let anyone come in the room. She won't let family come in, she won't accept any gifts or flowers, she won't answer the telephone; she is just lying there trying to die. If anybody ever needed a minister, Mrs. Davis in Room 858 needs one. Go to her."

It scared me to death. I didn't know what to say to Mrs. Davis in Room 858, who was facing surgery the next morning that she might not even survive, might not even make it off the operating table. So I started walking down toward her room, strategizing. I was young and thought I was supposed to strategize. I've learned since then that you don't do that; you just go love people. But I didn't know that then. I started strategizing.

Then I remembered nondirective counseling—I'd learned that in school. Nondirective counseling is when you let the other person talk and you just grunt every now and then. Or you repeat back what the person says: "I don't feel so happy today." You respond, "Oh, you don't feel happy today." And they just talk and talk, and you just grunt and listen and repeat, and after a while, that person just thinks you're great because you let them ventilate, and they go away happy and you're happy! So I decided, *I'll use nondirective counseling on Mrs. Davis in Room 858.*

I went on down the corridor toward her room, filled with confidence like a combination of John Wesley, Martin Luther, and Mother Teresa, all rolled into one. I was ready to do it! However, when I got to the door, I heard the pitter-patter of little feet behind me. I turned to see the head nurse running after me, and she said, "Oh, Jim! Wait a minute, wait a minute! I forgot the most important thing: Mrs. Davis is so critically ill that the doctors want her to be perfectly still and she is not allowed to speak."

Now, are you familiar with the word *discombobulated*? I was discombobulated! I promptly went into the room and did everything wrong. I pushed the door open too hard and it slammed against the wall. I went over and kicked the bed. (You are not supposed to do that!) I tried to talk to Mrs. Davis, and everything came out wrong. In desperation, I tried to pray and botched up the prayer. I left that room totally humiliated. I went straight to my car, and I sat in my car and felt so defeated. As if it were yesterday, I vividly remember taking my fists and hitting them on the steering wheel and screaming at God, "Why did you get me into this? I can't do this! I don't have what it takes to be a minister!"

I drove back to the seminary campus and went to see my advisor. Dr. Fred Gealy was a real smart man. I started telling him I needed to drop out of the ministry, and he said, "Jim, I'm real busy. Can you come back and see me next week?" He was buying some time.

The next Thursday, I went back to the hospital. I went up to the eighth floor of the neurosurgery ward, and I slipped into the nurses' station. I went a little early, because I knew they would be giving out the lunch trays at that time. I slipped in and looked down the list to see if Mrs. Davis had survived the surgery. I couldn't believe my eyes: There was her name! Mrs. Davis, Room 858, condition good. I was amazed!

I went down to her room and knocked on the door. Now, let me tell you, the week before, the room reeked of death—the drapes were pulled, no flowers, no cards, no gifts. But, this time, it was the total opposite. I heard somebody say cheerfully, "Come in!" I opened the door, and sunlight was streaming in, music was playing softly, and gifts and cards were all over the place. Mrs. Davis was sitting up in the bed writing thank-you notes.

I went over to her and said, "Mrs. Davis, you probably don't remember me." And she said, "Don't *remember* you? How could I *ever forget* you? You saved my life!" I turned around; I thought maybe someone else had come into the room! I said, "I don't understand. I felt so terrible—I did everything so wrong." She said, "That's just it. I felt so sorry for you!" She said, "You were so pitiful that I just wanted to hug you." She said, "I felt compassion for you, and it was the first time in months that I felt anything but self-pity; and that little spark of compassion made me want to live again." She said, "And now the doctors tell me it made all the difference."

I walked out of that room inspired! Here's why: I learned a lesson that day that changed my life, a lesson that turned my life around. Every Sunday morning when I walk toward my pulpit, I think of Mrs. Davis. Every time I have to go to a family to tell them some bad news, I think of Mrs. Davis. Every time I sit down to talk with a couple who are having trouble in their marriage, I think of Mrs. Davis. Here's why. From that experience with Mrs. Davis that day, I learned that I don't have to be perfect. I don't even have to be good. All I have to be is faithful. Just do my best, and trust God for the rest.

Do something positive with the stress in your life. Bring it to God, and God will give you the strength to turn your problems into opportunities.

Don't just try to escape the stress. Don't just try to endure the stress. Elevate the stress: Let it spur you to action. Use the stress to do something good for the cause of Christ.

Let me be honest and put it bluntly. If I never got under stress, I would never get around to accomplishing much. I would procrastinate. I would put things off. The stress serves as a friend to me. When crunch time comes, it makes me get with the program.

Remember the powerful words of the text in Matthew 11. Jesus says, "Come to me, all you that are weary and are carrying heavy burdens, and I will give you rest" (v. 28). Then Jesus adds, "Take my yoke upon you, and learn from me" (v. 29). A key word here is *yoke*. In a nutshell, it means "service" or "ministry." What Jesus is saying here is this: Put service to God and others first in your life. Let that be your number-one priority, and everything else will fall into place for you. Redeeming the stress, using the stress, letting the stress stir us to creative service for God—that is a key to Christian living.

Remember how the German theologian Dietrich Bonhoeffer put it. Talk about a stressful life. He had been captured by the Nazi Gestapo and placed in one of those horrible prison camps—death camps, as some people called them. In that horrible situation, Dietrich Bonhoeffer wrote these words: "Lord, whatever this day may bring, thy name be praised" (*The Healing Fountain*, ed. Betty Thompson [Nashville: The United Methodist Church, 1973]).

And how about the apostle Paul? He had been beaten and flogged and imprisoned and run out of town; he had been shipwrecked and had suffered from exposure while adrift at sea; he had been stoned and robbed and scourged and criticized. Talk about stress! And yet through it all, he could say, "Bring it on. I'm ready for anything, for Christ is my strength. Whatever you throw at me, I'm going to use it to serve my Christ. He is my Rock. He is my Fortress. He is my Strength. He is my Lord."

Can you say that and mean it? This is our calling as Christians, not just to escape the stress, not just to endure the stress, but instead to elevate the stress and use it to serve our Lord.

How does the Christian faith help us? First, claim the healing fellowship of the church.

Let the church family's arms of love surround you. Let the prayers, the casseroles, the tender handshakes, the gentle hugs, the letters, be means of strength. Get back into church as soon as you can and let the church be part of God's healing process.

Next, claim the new power that comes only from having gone through the grief pilgrimage. Those who have gone through sorrow have a new empathy, a new compassion, a new power to help others. The truth is that those of us who have walked through the valley of sorrow have a new strength of character because of that experience; this gives us a kinship with all who suffer and a unique ability to help them. So claim the healing fellowship of the church and claim that strength to help others which comes only from a firsthand struggle with sorrow.

And finally, claim the presence of God. This is what Jesus Christ came to show us—that God is with us and for us. He is a loving Father. Contemplate the story of the young man whose wife had died, leaving him with their small son. Back home from the cemetery, they went to bed early because there was nothing else he could bear to do.

As he lay there in the darkness—grief-stricken, heartbroken, numb with sorrow—the little boy broke the stillness from his bed with a disturbing question: "Daddy, where is Mommy?"

The father got up and brought the little boy to bed with him, but the child was still disturbed and restless and occasionally would ask a probing, painful question. "Why isn't she here?" "When is she coming back?"

Finally he said, "Daddy, if you face is toward me, I think I can go to sleep now." And in a little while he was quiet.

The father lay there in the darkness, and then in childlike faith, lifted up his own needy heart to his Father in heaven: "Oh God, the way is dark, and I confess that right now I do not see my way through. But if your face is toward me, somehow I think I can make it."

The good news of our faith is that God's face is toward us and he is with us.

Some months ago, just a couple of weeks before we left on our vacation, I began to have some pain in my lower back, and then the pain started running down the outside of my right leg. Macho-style, as men will do, I "toughed it out" for a while, but the condition became so painful that we had to come back from our vacation to see my doctor. He checked me over and took some X-rays, but they were not totally conclusive, so he sent me to a back specialist. I went to the back specialist knowing and dreading that he was going to say those three little initials I have come to dislike so much. Sure enough, he said them: "MRI."

Have you ever had an MRI, a Magnetic Resonance Imaging? They slide you into a tube and take magnetic pictures. The pictures are incredible, miraculous, wonderful, but the MRI experience is not wonderful for some people. Sixty-five percent of the population has no trouble at all, but about 35 percent of the people of the world have claustrophobia, and for those folks, MRIs are no fun at all. They are the pits! Unfortunately, not only am I in that 35 percent, I am near the top! I can get claustrophobic, *big time!*

Up to that point in my life, I had endured four MRIs. They all came when I was having my knee problems a few years ago, and after the last one, I said, "I will never do that again!" But then my new back doctor, who is a legend in his field, said, "Let's get you set up for an MRI. That will show conclusively what the problem is." I told my doctor about my last MRI experience, and he said, "Will you try it for me? If you can't do it, you will be in good company, but the pictures are so helpful. So would you try it for me? I'll give you some medication to relax you." I told him that I had tried that once before and it didn't help much, but, okay, for him I would try.

The next day, I showed up for my MRI filled with dread. My appointment was for 3:00 P.M. on that Saturday. My wife, June, and I got there at 2:30. I filled out the necessary papers, and they took me in early. I quickly took the oral medication they gave to relax me, knowing it would not have time to work. But when I got into the MRI room and lay down on that little bed that slides you into the tube, I looked at the clock on the wall—it was ten minutes till three—and suddenly, I felt this incredible sense of peace. They slid me into the chamber. I closed my eyes, quoted Scripture, said prayers, and I felt so peaceful.

Twenty minutes later, they slid me out, and—I can't believe I'm saying this to you, but—I could have stayed in there another twenty minutes! I came out to the waiting room and told June that I made it just fine, and she said, "You won't believe what happened. Richard came by, and we had a prayer for you." Richard is a layman in our church who makes hospital calls for us on weekends. He had finished his calls at Methodist Hospital and was cutting through the ER waiting room to take a shortcut to another hospital, and he just happened to see June sitting there. He asked what was going on. She told him about my MRI. Quickly, he said, "Let's say a prayer. An MRI can be claustrophobic, and I know how that is." And standing there in the waiting room, Richard and June held hands and prayed for me. I said to June, "What time was that?" And June said, "It was at ten minutes till three"—the precise moment I had felt that amazing sense of peace! I know some will say, "Aw, it was the medication," but I believe with all my heart it was the power of prayer!

You know, we all need that, don't we—the prayers of others, the prayers of those who love us. Having someone else pray for us is a beautiful thing, a powerful thing; but it's not enough. In addition, we need to have our own personal prayer life.

One night, a happily married couple were on a much anticipated trip to celebrate their twenty-fifth wedding anniversary, when their car slammed into a semi-trailer truck rig parked along the shoulder of the highway. They were both killed instantly in the grinding crash. Their three sons (ages twenty, seventeen, and sixteen) were left, in their grief, to open both anniversary cards and sympathy cards on the same day; to turn roses sent for a celebration into memorial flowers for a funeral; to take giant steps into adulthood by selecting caskets and burial spaces for their parents; and to cope with all the other details and decisions that are part of such a trauma.

The middle son, who handled most of the arrangements, testified how, in the wilderness of his confusion and grief, he had experienced more than once the powerful presence of God. He told his pastor that presently he saw God as his shelf, and although everything on that shelf had been moved around, changed or broken, the shelf had remained the same. He was discovering that the things he rests on the shelf will always change, but the shelf will not. Like the shelf, God is always the same.

God is always the same. We can count on that. And we can count on God! That son, though only seventeen, had already learned from his parents and his church how to trust God. Can you trust God like that? Are you limping along through life? Or have you learned how to walk in love and walk in trust?

It was obvious that the beautiful young woman sitting across the desk from me was deeply troubled. She was nervous, scared, grief-stricken, and heartbroken. And understandably so, because only a few weeks earlier, a tragic farm accident had, in a matter of seconds, made her a widow—a twenty-six-year-old widow with three preschool children. Her bright, energetic young husband had been so strong, so confident, so prosperous, so active, so full of life. But one morning his tractor had brushed against a hot electric wire! One minute, alive, vibrant—full of love and vitality and fun, with great hopes and dreams for his future and for his family—the next minute, gone!

Tears glistened in her eyes as she told me about his fatal accident. Her mascara smudged her cheeks just a bit from the constant dabbing at the corners of her eyes with a dainty handkerchief. The knuckles of her delicate hands were white as she twisted the handkerchief in her lap.

"I don't know how I'm going to make it without him," she said. "But I know one thing: I have a choice to make! I can get bitter or I can get better. And I have come to the church because I want to get better!"

I had never heard it put just that way before, but in a very special sense, she had underscored a universal truth in a crystal-clear way—when trouble comes, when life tumbles in around us, when disappointment breaks our hearts, when sorrow grips our spirits—*we have a choice: We can grow BITTER, or we can get BETTER!*

I once heard Ralph Sockman express it like this: "A grief is a sorrow we carry in our heart. A grievance is a chip we carry on our shoulder." All of us at one time or another must face trouble. It is universal and impartial, and not one of us is immune. There is no wall high enough to shut out trouble. There is no life, no matter how much it may be sheltered or protected, that can escape from it. There is no trick, however clever, by which we can evade it. Sometime, somewhere, maybe even when we least expect it, *trouble will rear its head, thrust its way into our lives, and confront and challenge every one of us!*

The psalmist did not say, "I will *meet* no evil." He said, "I will *fear* no evil." So the question is not *Will trouble come to me?* It will! The question is, *How do I respond to the troubled waters?* The choice is mine, and the option is clear: *Will I let this trouble make me bitter? Or will I, with the help of God, use it to make me better?*

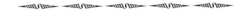

65

His name was Nodar Kumaritashvili. He was just twenty-one years old. The nation of Georgia was so proud of him. He was one of their most promising young athletes. They had hoped to watch him represent his country well and vie for a medal in the 2010 Winter Olympic Games in Vancouver. But, instead, they gathered on a Saturday morning to mourn his loss, after the young luger was thrown to his death in a practice run on the Olympic luge track just hours before the opening ceremonies.

Nodar lost control of his sled during a training run, shot off the course and slammed into a trackside steel pole at nearly ninety miles per hour. The following Saturday morning, thousands of mourners gathered in the yard of his family's two-story brick home in Bakuriani, Georgia, for a traditional funeral feast.

Inside the house, Nodar's body lay in a coffin, surrounded by Orthodox Christian icons, burning candles, and stunned, heartbroken family members and friends. A small choir sang chants, and a portrait of the handsome young athlete hung on the wall. Nodar's father, David Kumaritashvili, stared at the portrait and with tears glistening in his eyes, he said: "I wanted to throw a wedding feast for you. Instead, we have a funeral."

A few days later young Nodar Kumaritashvili was laid to rest in the cemetery of a tiny church in that beautiful mountain village where he grew up and trained for years to become an Olympian.

He was so young and so talented, with high hopes, big dreams, and great expectations. So perfectly conditioned, so full of life— and then so quickly gone!

Nodar's story is a harsh, sobering, and dramatic reminder of how hard life can sometimes be, and how fragile! The stark reality is that the tough and painful problems of life can so suddenly rise up and knock us flat. Sometimes when we least expect it, the world can take the wind out of our sails.

What do we do when that happens? What do we do when the hard knocks of life tumble in on us and threaten to tear us apart? How do we respond to the troubles of the world?

Do we try to run away and hide? Do we just quit on life, throw in the towel, feel sorry for ourselves, and wallow in self-pity? Do we retreat into a hard shell of cynicism, forever bitter and angry at the world and everything and everyone in it? Do we go through the rest of our life with a chip on our shoulder, ready to fight at the drop of a hat? Do we look for someone to blame it on? Do we blame it on God?

No, there is a better way, and the Scriptures remind us of that over and over again. Remember how the psalmist put it: "Yea, though I walk through the valley of the shadow of death, I will fear no evil: for thou art with me" (Psalm 23:4 KJV).

The apostle Paul knew well the problems, the challenges, the dangers, and the heartaches of this world and remember how he said that nothing (not even death) "will be able to separate us from the love of God in Christ Jesus our Lord" (Romans 8:39). The Scriptures tell us boldly and repeatedly that the good news of our faith is that God is always with us with gracious love and redeeming power. So we don't have to "run scared" through life. In our joys and sorrows from the cradle to the grave (and even beyond the grave), the good news is that God will be with us, giving us the strength we need when we need it.

So many times as a pastor, I have heard people in hard, tough circumstances say, "This is the hardest thing we have ever gone through, but we are going to make it because God is with us as never before." Notice those last three words, "as never before." Isn't that something? "God is with us as never before," they say. There are probably two reasons that people feel that way. First, when we are in those tough times, we are more open to God's presence and help; and second, when we are facing the hard troubles of the world, that's when God (like a loving parent) wants to be closest to us, his children, to help us and support us and encourage us.

I remember watching a storm develop on the Sea of Galilee during my first trip to the Holy Land. It came with amazing quickness and with no warning. One minute the sun was shining brightly, the winds were calm, and the water was still as glass. But then, out of the blue, the storm sprang up. Harsh gusts of wind began to blow, and in no more than fifteen minutes the sea was white with large foam-crested waves. Great billowing waves crashed on the shoreline, and over a hundred yards from the lakeside you could feel the spray of water kicked up by the storm. In just a matter of minutes, the still, glassy water and the clear blue sky had given way to a violent, raging storm.

Mark's Gospel (in chapter 4) records just such a storm, a storm that came with frightening suddenness and intensity. It lashed against the boat that was carrying Jesus and his disciples. The disciples, "scared out of their wits," rush to Jesus for help. Of all things, can you imagine this? He was sound asleep, resting peacefully on a pillow in the stern of the ship. He was completely at peace in the midst of a storm. There must be a sermon there somewhere.

The original Greek words here are vivid and they add greatly to the drama of the story. In the original Greek text the storm is called a *seismos,* the Greek word for "earthquake." *Seismos* gives us our word "seismograph," which is the instrument we use today to record the intensity of an earthquake. The implication is that the storm in Mark 4 was like an earthquake at sea.

Another interesting Greek word here is *kaluptesthai,* which means "completely hidden." The waves were so high that the boat was "completely hidden" as the waves crested and towered over it and tossed it to and fro.

The disciples were understandably terrified by this sudden turn of events. Only moments before, Jesus had been teaching from this boat as it sat calmly in the quiet and peaceful waters, but now the boat was being hurled about violently by the mad waves of the raging sea. "Wake up, teacher, wake up," they shout to him, shaking his shoulder with panic in their eyes. And then, just a bit irritated with him for being able to sleep in such dangerous circumstances, they question him: "Don't you care? We are all about to be killed here. Are you going to sleep through this? Don't you even care?" And then in his special way, Jesus rises to the occasion. He stands up and speaks out, and he calms the storm.

Helice Bridges, author and founder of Difference Makers International, a nonprofit educational foundation committed to providing school and community programs that create dignity and respect among all people, tells this story. Not long ago, a schoolteacher in New York called all of the children in her class forward and gave each one of them a blue ribbon imprinted with gold letters that read "Who I Am Makes a Big Difference." Then she told each student in turn what was special about each one of them and how each one made a big difference to her and to the class. To one student she said, "You have such a wonderful sense of humor, and you bring joy to our class." To another, she said, "You have such a curious mind, and you ask excellent questions that stretch our minds and help us grow." To still another, she said, "You are so kind to everyone, and your beautiful spirit inspires and encourages all of us" and on and on she went, praising each and every student.

The students were delighted. Then she gave the students some ribbons to take to other people out in the community and encourage them to do the same and keep it going. One student went to a junior executive who had helped him, and the junior executive in turn went in to see his boss, who had the reputation of being serious and grouchy. The junior executive sat down with his boss, told him about the project, and presented him with a blue ribbon. The junior executive said to his boss, "You are so brilliant! You have helped me so much, and you've taught me so much. You are a creative genius, and I appreciate and admire you more than words can express. You have made a big difference in my life, and I thank you."

The boss seemed very surprised. The junior executive pinned the blue ribbon on his boss, and then he asked the boss to take the extra ribbon and pass it on—to give it to someone who had made a big difference in his life. That night, the boss came home to his fourteen-year-old son and sat down with him. He said, "The most incredible thing happened to me today. I was in my office, and one of the junior executives came in and told me he admired me, and then he gave me a blue ribbon for being a creative genius. Imagine that. He thinks I'm a creative genius! Then he pinned the blue ribbon, which says 'Who I Am Makes a Big Difference,' on my jacket, just above my heart. He gave me this extra ribbon and asked me to find somebody else to honor.

"As I was driving home tonight, I started thinking about whom I would honor with this ribbon, and I thought about you. I want to honor you because you mean so much to me. My days are really hectic, and when I come home I don't pay a lot of attention to you. Sometimes I yell at you for not getting good grades in school and for your bedroom being a mess, but somehow, tonight—I just wanted to sit here and, well, just let you know that I love you so much and that you do make a big difference to me. You and your mother are the most precious persons in my life. You are great, and I love you!"

The startled boy started crying. He couldn't stop. His whole body shook. Finally, he caught his breath, looked up at his father, and said, through his tears, "Dad, I was planning to commit suicide tomorrow because I didn't think you loved me. Now I don't need to." (Copyright © Helice Bridges of Difference Makers, Del Mar, California.)

We don't have to limp through life. We can honor God by walking in love.

Maybe what we need most when we are hurt is a sympathetic ear, someone who cares enough to listen, encourage, support, and affirm.

My father died as a result of an automobile accident when I was twelve years old. I remember vividly the first day back at school after my dad's funeral, during recess, out on the school yard, telling my sixth-grade friends about the car wreck that took my dad's life. One of them asked, "Jim, does it bother you to talk about it?" I can remember as if it were yesterday how I realized (even as a twelve-year-old boy) that I needed to talk about it; I needed to reminisce, I needed to verbalize it, I needed to express it, I needed to talk it out.

Some years later, I also lost my mother in a car wreck. I wrote and preached a sermon about that experience and the accompanying grief. People asked, "How could you do that?" Well, I needed to do that. It was therapeutic for me. It helped me to talk it out. My heart was broken and I needed to talk about it.

When I first started out in the ministry, as I would work with people in grief, I thought it was my job to talk, to explain, to interpret. I thought I was supposed to give them answers. But now I do just the opposite. I let them talk, I encourage them to talk. I know now (because I have been through it personally many times) that what people in sorrow really need is a listener. So I say: "Tell me about it. Tell me what happened. Let's reminisce together about your loved one. Let's remember together his or her best qualities."

So, when your world caves in, when your heart is broken, find a friend with a sympathetic ear—and talk to them. Talk it out; it really helps.

It also helps immensely to talk it out with God. That's what prayer is. It is "friendship with God" and that's what friends do. They talk it out. So, feel free to talk to God and tell God honestly and openly and candidly what you are thinking, what you are feeling, and what you are needing. God will always be there for you and God will always hear you with love and understanding and compassion. God is the one who can hear your cries and give you the strength you need.

———————————————————

A couple of weeks ago I had a important moment of penitence. It had been one of those days—hectic, frantic, with one emergency after another all morning long and into the afternoon. Ten minutes before an important meeting, I was driving down the street when I suddenly felt weak. I realized that I had been so busy I had missed both breakfast and lunch, so I decided to stop and pick up a quick sandwich.

I went into a small carry-out establishment and ran into the slowest sandwich-maker west of the Mississippi. I ordered a turkey sandwich, and a sweet little lady started to create it. She would pick up a piece of bread and smile at me and nod. I would smile and nod back. Then she would begin to spread the mayonnaise. She worked with that sandwich so slowly I began to pace. I cleared my throat nervously and looked at my watch impatiently, but to no avail. She would not hurry.

Finally my patience wore thin. I decided I simply couldn't wait any longer, so I raised my hand to wave to her to just forget the sandwich.

At that moment, she looked at me, "Sir, may I ask you a question? Don't you work at St. Luke's Methodist Church?"

"Yes, ma'am," I answered.

"You're Jim Moore, aren't you? The minister at St. Luke's?"

"Yes, ma'am."

"I can't believe this," she said. "My husband will be so thrilled to know you were here. You see, we watch your service on television every Sunday, and we just love your church. Your choir is wonderful, and we even like your sermons. My husband had a stroke about a year ago, and the highlight of his week is Sunday morning when your church service comes on. Would you sign this napkin so I can show him that you came in?" Then she added, "By the way, were you about to say something?"

I replied, "I was just about to say that you certainly do make a fine sandwich!"

I walked out of that shop with a turkey sandwich in my hand and a prayer of penitence in my heart: "O God, forgive me; help me to be understanding. Teach me to always be kind; deliver me from impatience."

It's easy to love those who are attractive to us. It's easy to love those who love us back. But unconditional love? Now that's something else. Love to all freely given, love expecting nothing in return, love with no strings attached, love even to those who hurt us. Only God's Holy Spirit can give us the strength to love like that; only God's Holy Spirit can enable us to love the way Jesus loved. Let me show you what I mean.

In the early 1980s, a young man from Lancaster County, Pennsylvania, went to Colombia to fulfill his lifelong dream. He had a mission heart and all of his life he had prepared himself to go to Colombia so he could translate the Bible into the native language there and share the good news of the Scriptures with those people. But in January of 1981, this young man, Chet Bitterman, was kidnapped by Colombian rebels. They beat him, shot and killed him, and left his body in a hijacked bus. Imagine how his parents and loved ones back in Pennsylvania must have felt because of the senseless and brutal death of this fine, innocent young man.

A year later, following the leadership of Bitterman's parents, the churches and civic groups in Lancaster County, Pennsylvania, decided to do a demonstration of international Christian goodwill. They raised money to buy an ambulance and then they gave the ambulance to the state of Meta in Colombia, the place where young Bitterman had been killed.

Bitterman's parents traveled to Colombia for the ceremony. They made the presentation of the ambulance. After the ceremony, a reporter asked the parents, "How could you do this? How could you reach out in love to these people after what happened to your son here?" Bitterman's mother said, "We came in love because we are Christians. We serve him who said, 'They'll know you are Christians by your love.' We are able to do this because God has taken the hatred from our hearts."

When we are able to forgive, and when we are able to love unconditionally, it's because the Holy Spirit is within us.

CHAPTER FIVE

STORIES OF FORGIVENESS

It was a cold and snowy night in January. On the floor of the hospital where Nurse Sue Kidd worked, things were pretty quiet. She stopped by room 712 to check on a new patient, Mr. Williams. Mr. Williams had been admitted with a heart attack, and he had seemed restless and anxious all evening. He perked up when the door to his room opened, but then looked disappointed to see Sue walk in. He was obviously expecting, hoping, for someone else. As Sue checked Mr. Williams's chart and asked about his condition, she sensed that he wanted very much to ask her something. Finally, with tears in his eyes, Mr. Williams asked Sue to call his daughter and tell her about his heart attack. His daughter was the only family that Mr. Williams had left now, and he seemed very anxious that she know of his condition.

Sue patted Mr. Williams's hand and promised to call his daughter right away. Before Sue left, Mr. Williams made another request: Could he have a piece of paper and a pencil? Sue took care of that and then went directly to the phone to call his daughter. When Sue reached Mr. Williams's daughter, Janie, with the news of her father's heart attack, she was startled by the young woman's reaction. Janie screamed, "No!" In a panic, she asked, "He's not dying, is he? Tell me he is not dying!"

In her distress, Janie blurted out that she and her father had

75

not spoken in a year. They had gotten into a heated argument over Janie's boyfriend. It had been an ugly scene, with a lot of hostility and anger and tension; Janie and her father had not communicated since. Janie had stormed out and had refused to speak to her father. Her last words to her father had been "I hate you!" Of course, she hadn't meant that, and she had regretted having said it. All of this time, she had wanted forgiveness, and now a year and more had passed.

After reassuring Janie the best she could, Sue hung up the phone and began to pray. If only God would allow Mr. Williams and his daughter to reconcile! Her heart was so burdened by her phone conversation with Janie that Sue felt an urgent need to rush back to Mr. Williams's room to check on him. She found him unconscious, suffering from another heart attack. Within seconds, Sue's "Code 9" alerted the staff, and doctors and nurses filled the room in an attempt to save Mr. Williams; but it was too late. No amount of medical attention would restart his heart. He was gone.

As Sue walked into the hallway, she saw a doctor talking to a young woman. Shock and grief and panic mingled on the young woman's face. It was Mr. Williams's daughter, Janie. Sue ushered her into a lounge area and tried her best to comfort her, but Janie kept saying, "I never hated him. I loved him. I tried to get here in time to tell him, but now it's too late. Why was I so stubborn? Why was I so prideful? Now it's too late."

Janie wanted to see her father. Sue took her to his room. Janie leaned over her father's lifeless body and hugged him, and she cried painful tears.

Suddenly, Sue noticed something on Mr. Williams's nightstand: a piece of paper. Sue picked it up, and saw Janie's name was written at the top. Sue handed the note to Janie, and Janie read it out loud: "My dearest Janie, I'm sorry about that night. Please forgive me. Please know that I forgive you. Janie, I know that you love me, and I love you with all my heart. Don't you forget that. [Signed] Daddy."

Where grief and shock and panic had contorted Janie's features and filled her eyes just moments before, now, though there was grief still, there was also peace. The nurse, Sue Kidd, slipped out of the room and headed straight to the telephone to call her father.

If we could go back in time to Golgotha and gaze upon the cross that held Jesus' dying body, we would see a sign mounted above his head. On this sign, we would see the words: "This man is the Son of God." If we could only see the back side of this sign, we might also find these words: "My dearest [and our own names would appear], I forgive you. I know that you love me, and I love you with all my heart. [Signed] Jesus." And there would be this P.S.: "By the way, this is how I want you to forgive one another: I want you to live daily in the spirit of reconciliation and forgiveness." (Adapted from *Dynamic Preaching* [September 1998]: 21-22.)

Well, how is it with you right now? Do you hold onto your grudges? Store up your hurts? Harbor your grievances? Look for a chance to "get 'em back"? Or can people see in you Christ's amazing spirit of forgiveness?

Lewis Grizzard died some years ago and I miss him and his homespun humor. In his books and newspaper columns, he often wrote about growing up in Georgia. One of my favorites was his column in which he reminisces about growing up in a little Methodist church and how it was so dear to his childhood. His church was small and had to share its preacher with another congregation. On Sunday nights they had MYF: Methodist Youth Fellowship. When two brothers in town broke into a store, they were punished by being sent to MYF for six months.

The first night they were there, they beat up two fifth graders and threw a Cokesbury hymnal at the lady who met with the group and always brought cookies. She ducked just in time and then looked squarely into their devilish eyes. Then, soft as the angel she was, she said, "I don't approve of what you boys did here tonight...and neither does Jesus. But if he can forgive you, I guess I'll have to." She handed them a plate of cookies.

Lewis Grizzard concluded his column with these words:

> Those boys grew up and they're daddies now with steady jobs.... They rarely miss a Sunday at church. That was the first miracle I ever saw. It was the miracle of forgiveness. Now, if we could find that MYF leader today and say to her.... "How did you put up with those rowdy boys?" you know what she would say?... "Wasn't me. Left to my own devices, I would've poured the Kool-Aid on their heads and called the sheriff. But the spirit of Jesus was in me. It was the Holy Spirit within me that gave me the strength to forgive."

When we find the grace to forgive, it is simply because we are being carried by the presence and power of the Holy Spirit. Don't miss this: if you are unable to forgive, if you are having great difficulty forgiving someone who has hurt you or disappointed you, it may be a spiritual red flag. It may mean that you have drifted away from the spirit of God. That's number one. The Holy Spirit enables us to forgive.

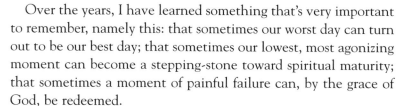

Over the years, I have learned something that's very important to remember, namely this: that sometimes our worst day can turn out to be our best day; that sometimes our lowest, most agonizing moment can become a stepping-stone toward spiritual maturity; that sometimes a moment of painful failure can, by the grace of God, be redeemed.

Have you ever heard someone say something like this: "That was a terrible experience, but in some ways it was the best thing that ever happened to me"? Let me show you what I mean.

It was a beautiful spring day, a day just made for playing baseball! Just a few weeks before, I had celebrated my twelfth birthday. At the time, baseball was my passion, my ambition, my life. I slept with my baseball cap on, I loved it so much.

I had a new glove, a new bat, a new ball, a new pair of cleats, and a brand-new Little League uniform. Our first game was that very afternoon at 4:00 at Hollywood Park. Our team was favored to win the league championship and to go on to the city finals.

I was primed and ready for action. I had everything needed to start the new season, except for one thing: I didn't have a plug of chewing tobacco! I had noticed on TV that some of the best Major League players always had a big chew of tobacco lodged firmly in the side of their mouth, making their cheeks puff out like they had the mumps.

I was determined to give it a try, and I was delighted later that morning when an older friend stopped by to wish me luck and to give me a big plug of chewing tobacco.

Now, my mother and father had warned me about chewing tobacco. They had said, "It's not good for you, and it will make you sick at your stomach!" I had heard their advice, and for many years I had heeded it; but now I was twelve years old, and I knew all about life (or so I thought), and I didn't think my parents really knew or understood the finer points of baseball.

So, I slipped out to the garage for my first (and last) experience with chewing tobacco. To my surprise, Mom and Dad were right: I got so sick, I must have turned green.

After I had suffered in solitude an hour or so in the garage, my dad found me. Painful though it was, I told him what I had done and blurted out an apology. He hugged me and said, "You stay here. I'll go get some medicine."

My appreciation for my dad grew by leaps and bounds that day, because he not only brought me the medicine but he also never told anybody what I had done that day. The medicine worked wonders, and soon I felt better physically; but spiritually and emotionally I was a wreck.

Embarrassed, I went straight to my room and sat there in silence, ashamed, sorrowful, scared, and penitent—genuinely penitent! I fell down on my knees beside my bed and prayed more fervently than I had ever prayed before.

The words were not high-sounding or theologically distinctive, but in many ways, it was one of the best prayers I ever prayed, just repeating, "O God, I'm sorry! I'm so sorry!"

Now, that was a terrible day, one of my worst moments. I shudder to think about it; and yet, in retrospect, it was one of my best days, because it brought me to God, it brought me to my knees, it brought me to my senses.

That day, as never before, I learned the meaning of penitence, and through the tender way my dad handled that situation, I learned that day as never before the meaning of grace and forgiveness.

Again and again, Jesus says this: God is a loving Father (not an angry, hostile, vengeful deity who must be appeased), a loving Father who cannot rest until he finds his lost children. This is the recurring theme of Jesus' teaching and we see this especially in Luke 15 in the parables of the lost sheep, the lost coin, and the lost son.

Interestingly, there are three different kinds of lostness depicted here: (1) the coin is lost by accident through no fault of its own; (2) the sheep is lost from wandering off, drifting away, going off on its own; (3) the son loses himself on purpose. He willfully, arrogantly, and pridefully runs away to the far country. But, in each case, the search is intense and victorious. And when the lost is found, there is great joy and celebration. Over and over the Bible teaches us this. We see it especially in the teachings of Jesus, the seeking, gracious, forgiving love of God! We love God because he first loved us.

His name was Ray. He had come to ask me a favor. His daughter (who was sixteen years old) was a teenage runaway, and someone had seen her in Dallas. He wanted me to go to Dallas with him. So we went to Dallas in search of her. All day, one place after another, we looked. I'll never forget the intensity in Ray's face, the sense of urgency, the conscientious, dedicated manner of the search, the hopefulness in his eyes as we went into arcades and discothèques and coffeehouses and teenage hangouts. "Maybe she'll be here," he would say. We looked and looked all day long and into the night, but we didn't find her that day.

On the trip back home, we rode along in disappointed silence. I'll never forget Ray's slumped shoulders and misty eyes, his agonizing unrest, because he was separated from his daughter. His child was lost, and he was heartsick. He wanted to find her and bring her home.

She surfaced a few days later in Washington, D.C. She had heard somehow that her dad was in Dallas looking for her urgently. She was touched by his love. She called Ray, crying. She wanted to come home. Ray was on the first plane to go get her and bring her back.

I learned something of what God is like that day with Ray—something of what Jesus taught in his parables about God's seeking love. God is a loving Father who desperately wants his children back. He wants to find them and bring them home. Nowhere is this more powerfully expressed than on the Cross at Calvary. "God so loved the world that he gave his only Son, so that everyone who believes in him may not perish but may have eternal life" (John 3:16).

However we put it, we stand in need of God's forgiveness to restore us to a vital and growing relationship with God, our Creator. And when we need forgiveness, human or divine, there is nothing we can do except ask for that forgiveness. But God, in Jesus, has already offered us forgiveness and restoration, even before we ask for it. God's grace takes the initiative and in Jesus we are forgiven. Grace is God's forgiving love—a gift from God to you.

There is a wonderful story of forgiveness about William and Catherine Booth, who were the founders of the Salvation Army. There was a young man named Alexander who had become active in the Salvation Army. William and Catherine had taken to the young man and liked him so well that he seemed almost like a son to them. He seemed so capable and trustworthy that they made him their financial officer to look after their funds. For a while, everything went along wonderfully and Alexander did a really fine job. But then one day it came to light that Alexander was actually embezzling funds from them, and huge sums at that. So he was arrested, convicted, and sentenced to prison.

But the first day he was permitted to receive mail, there was a letter to him from William Booth. The first day Alexander was permitted to have visitors, two people were there to see him, William and Catherine Booth. And every visitor's day, Alexander could count on two people being there to see him: William and Catherine Booth, the very people he had betrayed and hurt. When his prison term was finally over, he walked out of the prison, and they were there to meet him.

Catherine said to him, "Alexander, this is a great day! You're free, so let's go celebrate." She had packed a picnic lunch, and the three of them went over to a little park and had a picnic together. And when they were finishing, a really special thing happened. William looked at Alexander and said, "Son, Mrs. Booth and I have been doing a lot of talking and praying, and we have something we'd like to ask you to do." Alexander looked at him with a very surprised and startled expression as if to say, "What in the world could it be?" And then William reached into the picnic basket and pulled out a money bag and handed it to Alexander. "Son," he said, "Mrs. Booth and I would like for you to come back to work for us. We'd like for you to be our bookkeeper and our treasurer once again." That's grace, forgiving love!

William and Catherine Booth knew about grace, for they had experienced God's grace—God's forgiving love—and that day they shared it with Alexander. That's the kind of love, forgiving love, that God has for each of us.

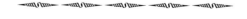

God knows where and when we need to forgive, and he sends the Holy Spirit to enable us to forgive. If we got in a time machine and went back to the day of Pentecost and said to Simon Peter, "Wow! What you did today was absolutely amazing. After what they did to Jesus you stood there and preached forgiveness with astonishing courage and conviction and grace. And your sermon was so powerful that 3,000 people came forward to join the church. How did you do that?" Peter would say, "It wasn't me. It was the power of the Holy Spirit."

If someone has done you wrong, and you are trying to find the strength to forgive all by yourself, all on you own, you are not going to be able to do it. It is the Holy Spirit that empowers us to forgive. When someone hurts us, we want vengeance! We want to get 'em back! We want to fight and show them a thing or two! That's our preferred reaction until we open our hearts to God. It is God who enables us to forgive, or, better put, when we forgive, it's not really us, it is the gracious Holy Spirit of God forgiving through us.

Blinded by law, we miss the love! That's what happened to the Pharisees' dealings when they criticized Jesus for healing, on the Sabbath, the man with the withered hand. They were so alarmed and so upset when they saw Jesus break the Sabbath law that they were completely blinded to the compassionate and wonderfully loving thing that he had done! He had helped a man, healed a man, changed his life, and they didn't even see it. They were blinded by their rules. They were blinded by their laws. Blinded by the law, they missed the love! "Surely the Lord was in that place—and they did not know it." Let me bring this closer to home with a true story.

It happened in a Southern city just a few years ago. Steve and his wife, Trudy, were building a new home on the lake. Late one afternoon as they were inspecting the progress on their new house, they heard their daughter's screams from the water's edge, where she had been playing. Their daughter Allison had been bitten by a three-foot-long copperhead snake! There was no phone, so there was no way to call an ambulance. So Steve and Trudy did what you and I probably would have done. Time was of the essence, so they scooped Alison up into loving arms, jumped into their car, and made a mad dash to the nearest hospital. With the car's emergency flashers on and the horn blasting, they drove frantically through the streets in search of medical help for their daughter. It was a horrifying, life-or-death situation. Finally, they arrived at a hospital and rushed into the emergency room, where a talented team of doctors and nurses worked with care and precision (over the next seven days) to save Allison's life.

But when her father came out of the emergency room, he was met by a police officer who ticketed him for five traffic violations—speeding, running a red light, running a stop sign, reckless driving, and disturbing the peace—and he was put on probation.

This story shows vividly the weakness of legalism. Now, please don't misunderstand me. I'm not fussing at the law. I know that we have to have laws. I'm not criticizing that police officer. He was simply doing his duty as he saw it. I am simply saying that there are times when human need must transcend the law. There are times when love and understanding and compassion must supersede the law. I'm glad that Jesus was a child of grace and a servant of love rather than a slave of law. Sometimes, blinded by the law, we miss the love.

Over and over again, Jesus liked to drive home a significant point by using the technique of contrast. Let me show you what I mean.

For example, in the parable of the prodigal son (Luke 15:11-32), the gracious love of the forgiving father is seen all the more powerfully as it is contrasted with the rigid, unbending bitterness of the elder brother.

In the parable of the Pharisee and the publican (Luke 18:9-14), the genuine humility of the publican is underscored more dramatically as it is set alongside the self-righteous arrogance of the proud Pharisee.

Also, the terrible plight of the poor man Lazarus (Luke 16:19-31) is shown even more graphically as his situation is compared to that of the indulgent rich man who is commonly known as Dives.

In chapter 20 of Matthew we see it again, a fascinating contrast of personalities: the gracious and generous householder, over against the angry, resentful day laborers. But wait a minute; we are getting ahead of ourselves. The truth is that this parable is very perplexing and troublesome to many people, especially at first reading, and they (like the angry day laborers) cry out, "Unfair! Unfair!" Well, let's remember the parable together, and then let me give you a couple of keys that I think will unlock this story and enable us to learn the important truth Jesus intended to communicate through it.

The parable actually describes fairly well the kind of thing that happened each September in first-century Palestine. The grape harvest ripened toward the end of September, followed closely by the rainy season. It was urgent to get the grapes in before the rains came or else there would be extensive damage to the crop, and a big financial loss. More often than not, it was a frantic race against time. Any worker was welcome, even if he could give only an hour or so to the job.

Since this work was obviously seasonal, the householder did not have a regular crew of workers on hand to harvest the grapes. Rather, at just the right moment, he would go into the marketplace to find workers he could hire for the day to bring in the crop.

Now, the going rate for this kind of day labor was a *denarius*. That was not much money—about twenty cents in silver. Not

85

much, but enough to buy food for your family for the night. Any less than that wouldn't do much good. Today, it would be like going grocery shopping with a dollar; you just can't feed your family for that. Why, I went to the supermarket the other day, got to the checkout counter, and discovered that I had bought $87 worth of stuff and still had nothing to eat! If a worker back then went home with less than a *denarius*, he would have a worried wife and hungry children. And the householder in this parable knew that!

The story begins as the householder senses that the harvest time is at hand, and so he goes out early in the morning to hire workers. The workers agree to work for him that day for a denarius (the usual rate), and he sends them to the vineyard. Later that morning (about 9:00) he realizes that more workers are needed. So he finds some more hands and sends them to work also, promising to pay them what is right. Twice more (at noon and at 3:00 P.M.) he does this. Throughout the day, he continues to put more and more workers in the vineyard to gather the grapes. It's getting more urgent now. The daylight hours are slipping away so quickly. It's urgent to get the crop in and get it in rapidly.

Still later, very late in the workday, at "the eleventh hour," which means about 5:00 P.M., he gets desperate. Maybe he sees a cloud on the horizon; maybe it's a Friday and all work will soon have to stop for the Sabbath. Whatever the case, he knows that every second is precious now; every worker he can get is needed and time is a-wasting. So even at this late hour, he sends even more workers into the vineyard to help complete the harvest.

Finally, at the end of the day, he pays all the workers a full day's wage, a denarius. Those who had come early in the day are upset by this—irate, indignant, resentful. They march on the householder's house, chanting, "Unfair! Unfair!" And strangely at this point, the story reminds us of something we have heard before. Doesn't this sound like the elder brother in the parable of the prodigal son, who so bitterly resents his father's gracious treatment of the returning younger brother? He too shouts, "Unfair!" It's the same kind of situation, isn't it? "Unfair!" they cry.

But the householder responds to the workers who had been there from the beginning of the workday: "My friends, I did you no wrong. I paid you what we agreed upon. I gave you the fair going rate. Am I not allowed to be gracious to these others? I don't want their families to go hungry tonight. Do you? Do you really want to begrudge my generosity?"

Isn't this a great story? Perplexing at first; troublesome to many. But there are two significant keys here, two significant verses that unlock its great truth.

The first key is found in verse 1, indeed in the first seven words: "For the kingdom of heaven is like..." That's the clue. That's the key. You see, this story is not about labor relations, or fairness in the marketplace; it's about God and his kingdom! In this parable, Jesus is telling both his listeners and us that God's kingdom is not about laws and merit and earnings and privileges and benefits. No! It's about grace and acceptance and inclusiveness. It's about unconditional love. Whosoever will may come— even those who arrive late!

Now, let me bring this closer to home. Let me give you another hint: If you want to understand this parable better, just take it out of the setting of the vineyard, and apply it to the church. It means that those who join the church today are just as valid members, just as special, just as precious to God as those who joined forty years ago. And those who joined forty years ago will be the first ones to welcome them and accept them and include them, and to show them God's grace. "For the kingdom of heaven is like..." Those are the key words, because they remind us that this is not a story about today's workplace. It's a story about God and his kingdom, a story about God and his grace.

The second key that unlocks the story is in verse 15, where the householder says this: "Do you begrudge my generosity?" (RSV). Here is the point of the parable: God is forgiving, gracious, kind, compassionate, and generous, and he wants us to be that way too. He wants us to imitate his caring, loving ways.

The Gospels make it clear: The people who get cut off from God are those who begrudge God's generosity. The elder brother in the parable of the prodigal son missed the party. Why? Because he begrudged his father's generosity. The religious leaders of the first century got aggravated and outdone with Jesus. Why? Because he spent so much time with the outcasts of society. They begrudged his generosity.

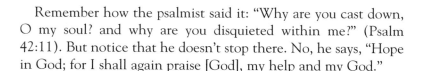

Remember how the psalmist said it: "Why are you cast down, O my soul? and why are you disquieted within me?" (Psalm 42:11). But notice that he doesn't stop there. No, he says, "Hope in God; for I shall again praise [God], my help and my God."

That's the answer, isn't it? For us to recognize that God is not some computer, off somewhere in the foggy distance. God is with us here. God is beside us now. God is within us. God is for us. God is our loving, forgiving Parent, and nothing can separate us from God and God's love.

Read the Bible closely and you will discover that the thread that holds it all together is the love of God. God loves us. God is with us. God will not desert us. God will save us and heal us.

I have a friend whose Bible is filled with notes in the margins. By some verses she has written, simply, "T. P." When asked what T. P. means, she says, "tried and proved."

When you feel depressed, nothing helps more than remembering that you can lean on God and God's love and strength. You see, it's "T. P." It's tried and proved!

CHAPTER SIX

STORIES OF GOD'S GRACE AND POWER

Some years ago, I attended a workshop at Lake Junaluska in North Carolina. The closing worship service ended with a moving responsive reading. The responsive reading, written by Charlene Anderson, was in the form of a dialogue between God and the worshipers. As the dialogue begins, God is calling us to serve him in the deep places of life, and we are responding to his call (at first) with some fear and anxiety. But God keeps reminding us of his strength and dependable presence, assuring us that he will always (in every circumstance) be there for us. God calls us to come on out into the deep water, but we make our excuses: We are not great swimmers. We are not sure we can make it that far. There might be a dangerous undertow that will sweep us away. Our feet can touch the bottom where we are now. We feel safe and secure in this shallow place. But we are afraid and uncertain to heed God's call to us to come out farther because the deep belongs to God. And still we procrastinate and hesitate. We feel inadequate. We feel all alone. God reassures us that we can do it and then says: You are not alone. I am with you. And the dialogue ends as we say in faith: OK, Lord, here we come!

Some years ago, there was a man who grew up in a mill town. He had wanted to go to college, but he came from a modest home and when he finished high school there was no money available for college, so he took a job at the mill.

This man and his wife had a son. He was an only child, and the man was determined to send his son to college. He wanted his son to have a better life and he knew the answer was college. So the day his son was born, the man placed a pickle jar on the floor beside the dresser in the master bedroom. Each night when he got ready for bed, the dad would empty his pockets and toss his coins into the jar. He did this every night for years and years.

When the jar was filled, the dad would sit at the kitchen table and roll the coins before taking them to the bank. Taking the coins to the bank was a big production, and when his son grew a little older he always got to go along with his dad on the trip to the bank. "These coins are going to send you to college someday," the father would say to his young son. "I want you to have a career. It's too late for me, but these coins are going to help you have a better life."

Each time as the dad slid the box of rolled coins across the bank counter toward the cashier, the dad would grin proudly and he would say, "These are for my son's college fund. I didn't get to go to college myself, but my son is going when the time comes. I'll see to that." Then father and son would celebrate at the ice-cream parlor. The son always got chocolate and Dad always got vanilla. When the clerk at the ice-cream parlor handed the dad his change, the dad would show his son the few coins nestled in his palm. "When we get home, we'll start filling the jar again," Dad would always say.

The dad always let his son drop the first coins into the empty jar. As they rattled around with a brief happy jingle, the father and son would grin at each other. "You'll get to college on pennies, nickels, dimes, and quarters," Dad would say. "But you'll get there. I promise you that."

The years passed and the son did go to college. He did well, graduated, and took a fine job in another town. Once while visiting his parents, he went into the master bedroom to make a phone call and noticed that the pickle jar was gone. It had served its purpose and had been removed. A lump rose in the son's throat and he stared at the spot beside the dresser where the jar had always stood. His dad was a man of few words, but through that pickle jar, the dad had taught his son the values of determination, perseverance, faith, and sacrificial love more eloquently than words could ever express.

A few years later, the son married a lovely woman named Susan, and he told her the story of the pickle jar and how it defined more than anything else how much his dad loved him. He told his wife that no matter how rough times were (even the summer when his dad was laid off from work for several months), not once would his dad take a single dime from that pickle jar. He would take on odd jobs to pay the bills but he would not touch the money in that pickle jar.

Some time later, the young son and Susan had a baby girl. They named her Jessica. The first Christmas after Jessica was born, they spent the holidays with the son's parents. After dinner, his mom and dad sat next to each other on the couch in the den and took turns holding and cuddling their first grandchild. Jessica began to whimper softly, so Susan took her from their arms and said, "She probably needs to be changed." She carried baby Jessica back to the master bedroom to change her diaper. When Susan came back into the den there was a strange mist in her eyes. She handed Jessica back to Granddad. She then took her husband's hand and led him back into the room. "Look," she said softly, her eyes staring directly toward a spot on the floor beside the dresser. To her husband's amazement, there (as if it had never been removed), stood the old pickle jar, the bottom already covered with coins.

The son walked over to the pickle jar, dug down in his pocket, and pulled out a fistful of coins. With a gamut of emotion choking him, he dropped the coins into the jar. Just then, he heard a noise behind him. He turned to see that his dad had walked into the master bedroom. His dad was smiling. His dad was holding baby Jessica. He had provided for his son. Now, he would provide for the one who followed his son.

Now, what does this story have to do with you and me? Actually, quite a lot because the story reminds us that God the Father (through sacrificial love) gave his Son the strength he needed—and he doesn't stop there. He also gives all those who follow the Son the strength, the help, the encouragement, and the support they need. This is the good news of our Christian faith: the Holy Spirit of God comes to give us strength and power, wherever and whenever we need it.

⸺⸺ ⸺⸺ ⸺⸺ ⸺⸺ ⸺⸺

One of the warmest memories of my childhood was something that happened to me when I was five years old. I had spent the day with my grandmother. Toward evening, a fierce storm hit. "Oh, Jim," my grandmother said. "How in the world are we going to get you home in this weather?" The answer came moments later as my dad walked in the front door. He had come to get me.

The storm showed no signs of letting up. The wind was blowing hard, rain was pelting down, lightning was flashing in the sky, thunder was rumbling behind the clouds. It was a dark and scary night. We didn't have far to go to get to our house, but the storm was nasty and getting worse. My dad had on a big, navy blue all-weather coat, and as we got ready to leave my grandmother's home, he said, "Jim, come under here." He covered me with his coat, he picked me up, and out into the storm we went.

Even though it was raining hard and the wind was howling and I couldn't see a thing under that coat, I was not afraid at all. Why? Because I knew my father could see where we were going.

So I just held on tightly and trusted him. Soon the coat opened and we were safely home.

Death is like that for the Christian. Grief is like that. The problems and challenges of life are like that too for the Christian. God covers us with his protective love. He holds us up and guides us through the storm. Sometimes in this life there is no way around it. We have to walk through the pain, the storms, the heartache. But the good news of the Christian's faith is this: we never walk alone. God is with us and he will see us through.

Have you heard about the man who fell into a deep manhole? He tried and tried but could not get out on his own, so he began to cry out for help.

A physician came by. He heard the man crying for help, so he wrote a prescription and tossed it down to the man. But the man was still in the hole.

A minister came by and heard his cry, so he wrote a prayer and tossed it down to the man. But the man was still in the hole.

Then the man's best friend came by. He too heard the man's cries, and (would you believe it?) the friend jumped into the hole with him.

The man said, "Why did you do that? Why on earth did you jump into the hole with me? Now we are both stuck."

"No, we're not," said the friend, "because I know the way out!" This parable-story reminds us of how Jesus Christ jumps into the deep hole of our lostness and captivity so that he, in his love and compassion and amazing grace, can lead us out to freedom and new life.

That's the way Jesus Christ loves us—generously, sacrificially, graciously, unconditionally—and that's the way he wants us to love one another. And whenever and wherever we do that, we had better take off our shoes, because we are standing on breathtaking holy ground.

During the Vietnam War, a friend of mine went through four
horrendous years as a POW. To this day, he attributes his survival
to his faith in God. He tells of the awful abuse, the torture, the
cruel and inhumane treatment that he and others endured. And
he remembers what gave him the courage to hold on. Over and
over, he repeated those words he learned as a child in Sunday
school, words he had carried through his youth, words that
shaped his philosophy of life as an adult.

> Yea, though I walk through the valley
> of the shadow of death, I will fear no
> evil: for thou art with me. (Psalm 23:4 KJV)

> [Nothing] will be able to separate us from the love of God in
> Christ Jesus our Lord. (Romans 8:39)

The great biblical promise of God is to always be with us. That
promise kept my friend alive and sane and hopeful. The advance
spiritual preparation in his life served him well and saved him in
the time of storm. No question about it, life is uncertain. We
need to prepare ahead to face the storms that are certain to come.

Some years ago, when I went off to seminary, I won some
scholarships. The scholarships helped a lot with my school
expenses, but the money was not nearly enough to pay for
tuition, books, fees, food, and room and board. So I had to work.
In addition to being a full-time theological student, I pastored
two churches and I was a janitor on the seminary campus.

It was in the janitorial job that I met a wonderful man, Mr.
Johnson. He was in his late seventies at the time, and he was my
immediate supervisor. Three first-year students were assigned to
work under Mr. Johnson in the care and cleaning of a large building on campus. None of us students knew anything about janito-

rial work, and the truth is we were all in our early twenties, so we weren't that interested. We had all kinds of ideas about the Bible and theology and sports and fast food, but we were real rookies when it came to the care and maintenance of buildings. Mr. Johnson decided to teach us, and he taught us a lot. Actually, we found out later that there is a lot more of that kind of work involved in being a pastor than we realized. With genuine respect, Mr. Johnson called each of us "Mister," but when he wanted to give us a lesson, he would always say, "Boys, what do you see?" That meant he saw something that needed fixing, and more often than not, we didn't see anything. Then Mr. Johnson would point out the problem, such as a smudge on the window, a spot on the wall, or a stain on the floor, and he would say, "Boys, you can't fix the problem if you can't see the problem."

One morning I was assigned to wax and buff the floor in one of the main classrooms. I got down on my hands and knees and applied the wax, but when I got ready to buff the floor, the electric buffer would not turn on. It wouldn't do anything. Just then, Mr. Johnson walked by and saw that I was having a problem. "Mr. Moore," he said, "what do you see?" "I see that the buffer won't come on," I said. And then Mr. Johnson smiled and said, "Mr. Moore, I have been doing this kind of work for a long time now, and over my long years of experience I have learned that the electric buffer works best when it is plugged into the power source!" Then he walked over, plugged the buffer into the electrical outlet, and of course it started right up.

This is an appropriate parable for many people today, isn't it? God's power is available. God's strength is accessible. God's energy is at hand. God's presence is nearer than breathing. God's forgiveness is freely offered. But some lives just are not connected!

Some years ago, a dedicated journalist was exhausted. He was at the breaking point. He was physically tired, emotionally drained, under severe nervous strain, confused, perplexed, stressed out, not knowing which way to turn concerning some highly important decisions he had to make.

He was staying at a friend's home prior to speaking at a big meeting. His friend said to him, "My friend, you look tired. Would you like to escape all this chatter and rest in a room upstairs?" The journalist said that he would like that very much.

To his delight, he was led to a beautiful, peaceful room. A fire was burning in the fireplace, an easy chair was drawn up near to it, and at his elbow was a little table with a Bible on it.

The Bible was open to Psalm 59, and in the margin opposite verse 10, someone had written in pencil a fascinating interpretation that kindled his mind and warmed his heart (as it does my own). In the King James Version, the first portion of Psalm 59:10 reads like this: "The God of my mercy shall prevent me." Let me hurry to say that in old English, the word prevent means "to go before." So the verse means, "The God of my mercy goes before me." But the interpretation penciled into the margin read like this: "My God in his loving-kindness shall meet me at every corner."

The journalist said that when he read those words, the message came to him as light in a dark place, light from the very heart of God. It lifted him, consoled him, encouraged him, revitalized him, and gave him the strength and courage to make his decisions and to do what had to be done. It was, for him, a moment that took his breath away.

"My God in his loving-kindness shall meet me at every corner." That is our faith, our hope, our confidence. That is the overriding theme of the Bible.

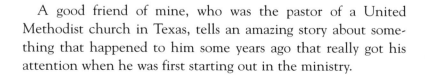

A good friend of mine, who was the pastor of a United Methodist church in Texas, tells an amazing story about something that happened to him some years ago that really got his attention when he was first starting out in the ministry.

The population growth of Dallas was moving rapidly and people were just flocking into neighboring areas, and my friend realized (as more and more people came into their church) that they needed to start a building program and expand quickly. He met with the architects, and they came up with a great plan that would ensure the long-range future of their church. Then he went to the bank to arrange the loan they would need. The banker wrote a number on a piece of paper and handed it to him, and then he said: "We will give you the loan if you will first raise that amount of money by such-and-such date. If you come back with one penny less than that amount, we won't even talk to you."

So the pastor and the leaders of the church went to work to raise that seed money: $500,000. And on the night before the deadline, they counted what they had raised, and they were exactly $14,000 short. My friend was so depressed. He sent everybody home, and he sat there at his desk (in the dark of the night) feeling blue and defeated. They had done everything they knew to do. They had left no stone unturned. They had worked so hard to raise that seed money, and then came the reality check: they were $14,000 short.

He sat there in his office wallowing in self-pity and feeling down in the dumps. How was he going to tell the board? How was he going to explain this to the congregation? Then, there was a loud knock at the door, and in came Phil. Now, Phil was the last guy in the world that my friend wanted to see in that moment; he didn't want to see anyone in that moment.

But in came Phil (and my friend groaned inside). "Well, Brother Mike"—Phil insisted on always calling him *Brother Mike* even though my friend protested—"I understand we came up short on the building campaign." "Yes, Phil, we are $14,000 short, and I don't know what to do about it!" "Well, I do, Brother Mike. We are going to pray about it, Brother Mike!" My friend said, "Holding hands with a man in my office in the middle of the night is not my favorite thing to do." But Phil persisted and he began to pray fervently: "O Lord, help Brother Mike. Be with Brother Mike and give him strength. Enable Brother Mike to find this money we need so desperately for our church. Let someone out there rise up and bring Brother Mike the help he needs."

Finally, Phil finished his prayer and left. My friend sat back down and began to worry and stew and fret about what to do. About five minutes later, the phone rang. It was a doctor in the community. The doctor said, "I understand you folks are trying to raise money for a new building for your church. I'm not a member yet, but I think we need a good strong Methodist church up here, so I would like to help. I have had a good year, and I want to give some of my good fortune to some worthwhile cause and about five minutes ago it hit me: there's no better place to give money to than a church. So I have written out a check to your church and if you're going to be there I'd like to bring it to you right now."

A few minutes later the doctor arrived in the pastor's office and handed him an envelope. My friend thanked him. They visited a few minutes and then the doctor left. He opened the envelope and—are you ready for this?—there was a check in there for exactly $14,000! My friend was so excited and he grabbed the phone to call Phil, and he said, "Phil, this is Brother Mike!"

My friend now looks back at that experience as a kind of rebirth experience, which gave him a new appreciation for Phil, and a new understanding of the power of prayer. He felt so down and out, so discouraged and defeated, but then suddenly (out of the blue) he felt reborn!

A good friend of mine had a traumatic experience a few summers ago that dramatically changed his life. John was on vacation with his family on the Atlantic coast near Savannah, Georgia, when it happened. Swimming alone one day at high tide, he was hit by a huge wave and knocked unconscious for a few moments. When he came to a bit, he realized that he was facedown, underwater.

The force of the wave had knocked him in toward the shoreline, and the water there was not very deep, but he was paralyzed. It turned out to be a temporary paralysis, but he didn't know that at the time. He only knew that he was facedown, underwater, and unable to move. Can you imagine that?

John thought to himself, "This is it! This is how it all ends for me! I'm going to die! I'm going to drown right here in the shallow waters of the Atlantic Ocean!"

Later, as he reflected on that moment, he remembered that he felt remarkably calm, and he had two thoughts. Today, he smiles about that and says, "Most people at a time like that would have more than two thoughts, but I've led a very dull life, so only two images came to mind."

First he thought, "My wife doesn't deserve this!" They had just gone through the horrendous experience of nursing their twenty-year-old son through the consequences of a terrible motorcycle accident that almost took his life, an accident that required extensive surgery and months of therapy and tender loving care. They were just coming out of that agonizing ordeal, and now here was John, lying paralyzed underwater in the ocean and thinking, "Jane doesn't deserve this."

His second thought was, "I've got a big job with lots of authority and clout and prestige, and I'm going to die here in the waters of the Atlantic Ocean. Somebody's going to get my job, and others will get nice promotions because of my loss. I'm creating slack in the job market!"

Just about then, a little boy playing in the surf stepped on John. The young boy ran to get his parents: "Mom! Dad! Come quick and help me! There's a man drowning down there!"

Well, the initial reaction of the parents was (how shall I say this?) parental! They were resting and reading under their beach umbrella and didn't want to be bothered. They didn't believe the little boy. They tried to dismiss him with a wave of the hand. "Now Billy, that imagination of yours! Nobody's drowning. Go on and play. Don't disturb us. Go play in the water or build a sand castle."

But bless little Billy's heart! He would not be put off. He urgently grabbed his parents by their hands and literally pulled them down to where the surf was pounding against the beach and John was drowning. Billy and his parents pulled John out of the water and the mother ran for help.

Later John would say, "What a message! I was saved by the love and concern of a little child. A little child shall lead them." The lifeguard administered CPR and revived John.

"As I came back to consciousness," John said, "I remember hearing voices as if they were way off in the distance, repeating something over and over. Then I heard the lifeguard saying, 'John, can you hear me? John, can you hear me?'"

John was rushed to the hospital. He was in intensive care and on life-support for several days. But now, because of the active, persistent love of a six-year-old boy; because of the expert work of a well-trained lifeguard; because of the commitment and diligence and wisdom of good doctors and nurses; because of the love, support, and prayers of his family and friends; and because of the miracle of God's grace and his healing touch, John is alive and well, active and healthy!

Now, let me tell you something interesting. If John were here with us today, he would say something that would at first sound startling. He would say, "I wish that wave had hit me thirty years ago, because that traumatic experience, horrible as it was, changed me! Strange as this may sound, it was the best thing that ever happened to me. It changed my life! It changed my values, my commitments, my concerns. It changed my priorities—and did they ever need changing! It drew me closer to my family. It taught me how to celebrate the preciousness of life. It brought me closer to God! Yes, I wish that wave had hit me thirty years ago!"

Now, why would John say that? For one reason and one reason only—because it was a life-changing moment. Let me ask you, How long has it been since you had a life-changing moment? A moment that touched you so profoundly, so powerfully, so deeply that you could never be the same again—a life-changing moment.

When he fed the five thousand, Jesus surveyed what resources were available, and he used them to solve the problem. Sometimes we fail to do this. The problem looms so large and seems so formidable that we suffer from tunnel vision, from narrow vision, from closed-mindedness, and as a result we are blinded to the available resources, the available tools, and the available opportunities. We don't even see them.

Some time ago, I watched Robert Redford's film *The Natural*, in which he plays a brilliant baseball player. (One man commented that this is the perfect movie for him and his wife: *he* loves baseball and *she* loves Robert Redford!) In *The Natural*, Robert Redford portrays an outstanding baseball player named Roy Hobbs, who is a naturally gifted athlete. At the age of nineteen, he is on his way to try out with the Chicago Cubs when he meets with misfortune and mysteriously disappears. Then, some fifteen years later, around the age of thirty-four, he shows up to play baseball for a fictional Major League team called the New York Knights. Roy Hobbs walks into the dugout with a five-hundred-dollar contract in his hand and reports to the manager, a crusty old baseball character named Pop.

The manager, Pop, thinks it's a joke. The Knights' players laugh and snicker at this thirty-four-year-old rookie named Roy Hobbs. A thirty-four-year-old rookie! This is unheard of. Rookies are nineteen, twenty, twenty-one—not thirty-four. Thirty-four is when many retire from baseball, not when they start. Pop tries to get rid of him, but Roy Hobbs won't leave. He has a contract. So they give him a uniform and put him on the bench.

Day after day, the New York Knights baseball team plays terribly. They get worse and worse. They can't hit, they can't field, and they can't score; they drop lower and lower in the standings. Then it's revealed that the manager, Pop, is in an awful predicament. He has a tremendous problem. In addition to being the manager, Pop is also one of the owners. Because the team is playing so poorly, attendance has fallen off, and the Knights are in a dire financial situation. Pop has had to borrow money from a mobster, and now he is in big trouble. His only hope is to win the pennant. If the New York Knights don't finish the season in first place, Pop will lose everything—his team, his job, his investment, and his place in baseball. Here Pop is, in this terrible situation. He is frustrated, worried, and scared; and he doesn't realize it, but he has the greatest baseball player who ever lived sitting on the bench.

Finally, they give Roy Hobbs a chance. They let him take batting practice. They throw him five pitches. He hits all five out of the park! Pop sees this available resource, and he puts Roy Hobbs in the lineup. Hobbs, with his great play, inspires the other players, and they begin to win. And they keep on winning, and they win the pennant. (The movie has a happy ending. I love happy endings!)

The point is that Pop made the mistake we often make. He didn't realize the available resource he had right there under his nose in the dugout. We get so blinded by the enormity or complexity of our problems that we don't see or use the resources that God has given us, that are waiting right at our fingertips.

Some years ago, a Roman Catholic priest was taken into captivity by terrorists in the Middle East; and he spent many horrible months as their prisoner. After his release, he told of the awful abuse and the inhumane treatment that he and others had endured. He had spent his life helping needy people and that's precisely what he was doing that day, when suddenly armed men came and captured him. They kept him in solitary confinement for weeks and weeks. One day, the captors tied explosives all over his body; and the priest was certain this was the end for him. Another day, the captors attached a chain to the ceiling of the priest's cell; and he was certain they were going to hang him. But these tactics were all designed to torture and intimidate him.

The priest told of how one day he was bound and trussed like a turkey, and shoved into a rack beneath a flatbed truck, where the spare tire is usually stored. Apparently his captors were taking him to a new hideout. But the priest felt certain that they were taking him out to kill him.

As he took that awful ride, he remembers what gave him the courage to face that moment. He kept saying these words to himself: *I am a human being of worth and dignity. I belong to God. I am redeemed. I am a child of God. He cares for me.* And over and over, he said the powerful words, "Nothing can separate me from the love of God in Christ Jesus our Lord; and nothing can separate me from him and his love" (Romans 8:38-39, paraphrased).

Then the priest prayed over and over these familiar words: "Yea, though I walk through the valley of the shadow of death, I will fear no evil: for thou art with me" (Psalm 23:4 KJV). Again and again, he spoke aloud the strong words of Jesus, "Lo, I am with you always." Later, he said, those promises of God to be with us in every circumstance kept him alive and sane and hopeful.

Now, it is very unlikely that any of us will ever have to go through that kind of traumatic experience, that kind of blatant abuse, but we all know what "the dropping-off place" feels like and how painful it is. But when it comes, when it happens, when we feel cast out to the uttermost parts of the sea, to the dropping-off place, the good news is that God will be there for us, even there with his special brand of love, grace, encouragement, and acceptance.

So that's number one: When you feel pushed by life to the dropping-off place, remember that God loves and accepts you, and that God will always be there for you. God in his loving-kindness will be there to meet us at every corner, even at the dropping-off places of life. I have found this to be so true in my own personal life. When I have had to walk through the valley of grief, every time, God was there for me. God was there for me at our dropping-off place, nearer than breathing and in ways that took my breath away!

Some years ago, in a small Mississippi Delta town, a man was driving a little foreign car when the back right wheel came off. When the wheel came off, it broke all four of the lug bolts that attach the wheel to the car. The man had a big problem. There were no lug bolts that he could buy in that small town. The closest parts store was twenty miles away. What in the world could he do? The police, the fire department, the mayor, and even the men playing checkers on the courtyard square gathered around, but no one could figure out what to do.

Then along came Crazy Leroy, as he was known. He was the town character. The townspeople called him Crazy Leroy because he sometimes did bizarre things and because he often didn't appear to be very bright. The men decided to tease Crazy Leroy, so they brought him over; showed him the car, the wheel, and the broken lug bolts; and asked him what he would do if it were his car. "Very simple," said Leroy. "The other three wheels have four lug bolts. I would take one off each wheel and use those three to attach this wheel, and then I would drive to Jackson and buy four new lug bolts." The crowd was amazed and they cheered for Leroy, and then they asked him how he figured that out. Leroy replied, "I may be a little crazy, but I'm not stupid."

It's amazing what you can do if you just use the things God's given you. Jesus found out quickly that the crowd had five loaves and two fish. He took what they had and used it to the best of his ability, and he trusted God—and God made it enough. God took the little and made it much. God took the little and made it work. God took the little and made it enough.

When we trust God and use what we have the best we can, God takes our little and makes it much. Jesus chose to cope rather than run, and he used the available resources.

Have you heard about the man who lived in a house by a river? Under the house, there was a light, airy cellar in which he kept his prize hens. But one night the river flooded his cellar, and the hens were drowned. Early the next morning he was off to his landlord to announce that he was going to move.

"But why?" asked the landlord. "I thought you liked the house."

"I do," said the tenant. "I like the house very much, but the river has flooded the cellar and all my hens are drowned!"

"Oh," said the landlord, "don't move on account of that. Try *ducks!*"

Now, that's a good Christian story because it reminds us that when one door closes on us, God will open another one. So when disappointment comes, be resilient. Bend a little, and then bounce back! Don't get bitter—get better! Let God, through the miracle of his grace, bring you through that valley and shape you into a better person—not a bitter person, but a better person.

When something goes wrong, one of the first things we want to do is find someone to blame it on! Look at the Israelites at the Red Sea. They see that cloud of dust on the horizon being kicked up by Pharaoh's army, and immediately they turn on Moses. Moments ago he was their champion, their leader, their hero; but now when trouble rears its head, they go for the jugular. "It's all your fault, Moses! A fine mess you've gotten us into. Why did we ever listen to you? You're the one to blame for this."

Some years ago I had a poignant experience while working with an alcoholic. He had been missing for more than a month. He left home drunk on Christmas Eve and staggered back on January 31. His wife, who had left him, called and asked me to check on him.

When I knocked on the door, I heard something crash to the floor inside. The man was stumbling around in a drunken stupor. I knocked again and called his name. I heard him fall to the floor and begin crawling toward the door. He fumbled with the door-knob, and when he finally pushed the door open he was lying facedown on the floor. He saw my feet, slowly turned his head upward, and found himself looking into the face of his minister. I guess at that moment, I must have looked ten feet tall.

He was dirty, covered with the filth of his own drunkenness, and had not washed or shaved or changed clothes for over a month. When he saw me, he began to cry.

I helped him up and got him on the couch. I washed his face and tried to get some food and coffee into him. Suddenly he turned on me and began to blame me for his problem. Then he blamed his wife, then his parents, and then he started in on his neighbors and those "hypocrites down at the church." He blamed the mayor, the President, and the Congress. He even cursed God for letting him be born.

He turned back to me. "Well, aren't you going to say anything?"

I answered, "I was just wondering whether there's anybody else we could think of to blame this on."

He looked at me angrily, and for a moment I thought I had

gone too far. But then he looked down, and after a few moments of silence, he said, "It's all my fault! I've made such a mess of my life, haven't I?"

"Well," I answered, "you are a mess right now, but your life is not over. You can start again."

He paused for a moment. "Jim, do you really believe that? Do you really believe God can help me whip this thing?"

And I said, "I surely do, but the real question is, do you believe it, and are you ready to do something about it? Are you ready to admit you've got a problem and need help?"

Evidently he was, because he went to A.A. And now with their help, with his church's help, with his family's help, and with God's help, he is whipping it. He called me the other day. He hasn't had a drink in almost twenty years. He knows he still has a problem. He is one drink away from big trouble. But he also knows he can't blame anybody else.

When we take responsibility for our own lives, our communities will help us, our families will help us, our church will help us, and God will help us. You see, the truth is, we don't need scapegoats. We have a Savior!

The great writer Mark Twain is, of course, most famous for his classic novels *Tom Sawyer* and *Huckleberry Finn*. However, in the late 1800s, he was also known as a popular lecturer as well as the author of several travel books. He got his start in the travel book area when he journeyed into the American West and as far as Hawaii. He then published informative and humorous articles about his trips, first in Western newspapers, and then national newspapers.

At a time when travel was slow, laborious, and difficult, Mark Twain was often away from home for long periods of time and his friends often did not know where to get in touch with him. One particular evening, a group of his friends realized his birthday was approaching. They wanted to send a birthday greeting, but they had no idea where he was, so they prepared a birthday letter; they all signed it, and then addressed it to:

Mark Twain
God Knows Where

A few weeks later, they got a response from Twain. He sent a note with just two words: "He did."

This is the good news. God knows where we are and what we need. He comes to us wherever we are to give us the help and power we need in that given moment.

CHAPTER SEVEN

STORIES OF GOD'S PEOPLE

Some years ago when we were living in Shreveport, Louisiana, a young man came down and joined the church at the end of our worship service one Sunday morning. His name was Tommy. He lived in a church-sponsored home just two blocks from the church. Tommy decided that I would be his friend, and we did indeed become good friends.

Tommy was quite a character. He had a sweet spirit, but he frightened some people because he looked different and talked really loud; and sometimes in his innocence, he would say embarrassing things or ask me embarrassing questions. He didn't mean to say things that most people would not say in public. He was curious and we were friends and he felt that he could ask me anything, and often he did ask me in the most public places in a booming voice.

He worked at a nearby hospital. He put the linens in the supply closets and could do his job well as long as nobody changed the routine. If the routine changed, however, he would become lost and confused and frustrated. If the door always opened toward him, no problem. But if someone changed the door so that it opened away from him, he could not figure that out. It would never occur to him to try it the other way. But Tommy was a good guy and a special child of God. He needed a friend, and I decided that I would be a friend to him.

Tommy's afternoon off work was Tuesday. He got off at 1:00 P.M., and he always came straight to my office. It was a standing appointment that he set. Every Tuesday afternoon at 1:15 he would show up at my office with pictures from a trip he had made with his parents, and he would show me his pictures.

Tommy's favorite thing to do was to sit in my chair behind my desk. He would pretend that he was the minister and that I had come to see him. He loved to sit in my chair and put his feet up on my desk and show me the pictures from his latest trip. His parents were well-to-do and took him to a lot of wonderful places.

Tommy and I had been friends for some five or six years when one day I heard that Walter Underwood had been elected bishop and that the church he had been serving (St. Luke's United Methodist Church in Houston, Texas) was open and that I was being considered along with many others to be appointed its minister. A few weeks later, the bishop called me to tell me that some folks from St. Luke's were coming to hear me preach the very next Sunday morning, and he said, "I want you to do three things: (1) don't tell anybody they are coming; (2) don't call attention to them in any way; and (3) preach a good sermon."

Well, I went to work on that sermon and when Sunday morning arrived, I was ready. After the 8:30 service, after everybody left the sanctuary, I was cleaning up the church and straightening things to get ready for the next service and looked up and saw this distinguished group of people walking down the aisle. I thought, "That's got to be the group from St. Luke's," and it was. We spoke, introduced ourselves, and one of them said, "We liked your sermon." I was surprised because I didn't even realize they had been there. I was expecting them in the 11:00 service. At least the pressure was off. So we just stood there having a nice visit, when all of a sudden, the sanctuary door flew open, and I heard somebody loudly call my name: "JIM!"

I recognized that booming voice—my worst nightmare. It was Tommy, just back from a trip to New Orleans. I was always glad to see Tommy, but not at that moment, because I had no idea what he was going to do or say as I was trying to put my best foot forward. He ran down the aisle and hugged me. I introduced him: "Tommy, these are some friends of mine from Houston. Have you ever been to Houston?" "Oh, yes," he said, "to the Astrodome and Astroworld and the Galleria. Once I got lost there, and my parents had to get the police to find me." Then he said, "Can I come and see you Tuesday like I always do at 1:15?"

"Sure."

"Can I sit at your desk and play like I'm the minister like I always do?"

"Absolutely. And Tommy, bring your pictures from your New Orleans trip and we'll look at them together."

While all this was going on, I was praying, "O God, please, please don't let Tommy say something embarrassing." Well, God must have heard my prayer because, amazingly, Tommy said, "Jim, I'll see you Tuesday, but now I'm going to get my seat on the front row and get ready for the worship service."

The St. Luke's group and I visited a while longer, and then they left. I breathed a sigh of relief. The next day, the bishop called me and said, "Jim, you must have done a good job because they liked you." And I thought, "I'm going to go home and frame that sermon!" But was I ever in for a surprise. Some weeks later, when I was sent to St. Luke's, I discovered that it wasn't my sermon at all. That group of people who came to hear me preach said, "Jim, do you know when we decided that we wanted you to be our minister?"

"Was it my sermon?" I asked.

"No," they said. "It was when Tommy came in!"

I learned a great lesson that day, namely this: The greatest sermons don't happen in a pulpit. They happen when we love other people. They happen when we love other people for God's sake. First, the Bible teaches us to love God because he first loves us. Second, the Bible teaches us to love other people for God's sake.

Only the Holy Spirit of God can build a church. Only the Holy Spirit can empower the church. Only the Holy Spirit can sustain the church. A church without the Holy Spirit is no church at all.

Have you seen the hit movie *Mr. Holland's Opus?* It's wonderful. It's the story of a dedicated music teacher named Glenn Holland. At the beginning of his career, Mr. Holland dreams of becoming a famous composer. He dreams of living in Hollywood and writing theme songs for movies, but he never gets to do that. Instead, he spends his entire career working with young students at John F. Kennedy High School.

With great tenderness, he works with a red-haired girl with pigtails who wants to play the clarinet, but no one believes in her. No one helps her; no one encourages her but Mr. Holland. With great compassion, he works with an African American student who wants to play the drums but has a terrible time finding the beat. With great patience, he works with a street-wise tough kid who has a lousy attitude and is down on the world. And Mr. Holland helps them all and hundreds more like them.

The conclusion of the film is a classic. Mr. Holland retires, and as he cleans out his music room at the high school, he tells his wife and his son that he feels like such a failure. He never accomplished his great dream; he never went to Hollywood; he never became a famous composer. With slumped shoulders, he heads out of the school, but then he hears a noise in the auditorium. He opens the door and sees that the auditorium is jampacked with his former students. They give him a long, thunderous standing ovation. They have come back to express their love and appreciation to this wonderful man who gave so much of his life to them.

Then the little girl with the red pigtails goes to the microphone. She's all grown up now, and, in fact, she is the governor of the state. She says, "Mr. Holland, we know that you never got to become the famous composer you dreamed of being, but don't you see? Your greatest composition is what you did with us, your students. Mr. Holland, look around you. We are your great opus! Mr. Holland, we are the music of your life!"

Our calling as a church is to be God's music to the world, to sing the song of forgiveness, to sing the song of love, to sing the song of the church's great faith. But we can't do that alone, and the good news of the Christian faith, the good news of Pentecost, is that we don't have to do it alone. God is with us. God is our strength, our guide, our provider, our inspiration, our comfort, our teacher. The Holy Spirit empowers us and enables us to forgive, to love unconditionally, and to build the church. And that's why God should do the driving, that's why God should be in the driver's seat, that's why God should be the number one priority in our lives.

On December 17, 1979, my mother died instantly in an automobile accident in Winston-Salem, North Carolina. The funeral was held in Memphis on December 20. We had to stay over a few days longer to handle some family and business matters. We flew back into Shreveport, where we were living at the time, on Christmas Eve, still very much in shock and grieving deeply.

Our plane landed at 3:30 that Christmas Eve afternoon. We drove to our home, put our luggage inside the house, looked quickly at the mail, and then headed for the church for the Christmas Eve Communion service. This was a very emotional moment for me—our first time back in our church since Mother's funeral. I will never forget what happened that night as long as I live. It was one of the most moving spiritual experiences of my life.

As I moved up and down the altar rail, serving the bread tray, people reached out and touched my hands. They didn't say anything—they just touched my hands. Even now, my eyes water as I think of it. This had never happened before nor has it since—hundreds of people just touching my hands, saying nothing verbally, but saying oh so much with the gentle touch of encouragement! It was a powerful moment for me. I had never felt more loved or more encouraged. Now, that is what the church is all about.

Whatever happens, we must keep on loving and keep on encouraging.

During the Los Angeles riots, an amazing act of love took place. A Hispanic man, Fidel Lopez, had been jerked out of his truck and beaten senseless by the rioters. He was being hit mercilessly with sticks and bats and bottles. He was being kicked repeatedly and battered with angry fists. A crowd of people stood by and watched.

Suddenly an African American minister, the Reverend Bennie Newton, came on the scene. Immediately, he ran, diving and covering Lopez's body with his own. He screamed at the wild-eyed mob, "Stop it! Kill him and you'll have to kill me, too!"

Bennie Newton turned back the rioters, and then he picked up the unconscious man and drove him to Daniel Freeman Hospital. Later, the Reverend Newton took up a collection at his church to repay Fidel Lopez the $3,000 the looters had stolen from him that afternoon.

Some days later, the two men met. They hugged each other and cried.

Fidel Lopez said to Reverend Newton, "How can I ever thank you? You saved my life! But why? Why did you do it? Why did you risk it?"

The Reverend Newton said, "Because I am a Christian. I believe in sowing love, not hate. I believe in helping, not hurting. I believe in Jesus Christ, the Prince of peace and love."

The Reverend Bennie Newton obviously practices what he preaches, and he obviously knows that the ligaments of love bind us together. They enable us to move, and they work best when exercised.

Some time back, I ran across a true story that underscores the point. A chaplain in World War II told of a Sunday morning on one of the islands south of Japan. It was time for worship and it was raining badly, so hard that one could hardly see through it. Despite the rainstorms, about one hundred men gathered in the mud and the mire. This chaplain shouted over the noise of the rain and wind, "Do you want to have worship service today?" To the man, they all said yes. So they hummed some familiar hymns because they didn't have hymnbooks. They recited the familiar words of the twenty-third Psalm because they had no Bible. The chaplain said, "The rain was beating down on my steel helmet and the water was coming off, and I could hardly see them. I asked them, 'Do you want me to preach?'" Standing in the rain, ankle-deep in mud, the men answered back, "Yes, preach." So for twenty minutes, the chaplain preached to those men and they listened intently.

The chaplain later said that he came back to the civilian pulpit, where people sit in cushioned pews and air-conditioned comfort, where there are those who feel that to come two blocks to church is a very painful thing to do. Why is it that a worship service over there in the mud and mire means more than worship in a beautiful church sanctuary sometimes? The answer is simple: those men on that rain-soaked island knew that they were facing the possibility of death at any moment, and they needed to be reminded that the God they put their faith in and trusted their lives with was bigger than the world, bigger than the war, bigger even than death, and as long as they put their trust in God, all was well.

We need to remember that week by week. So when times are hard, keep on keeping on; keep on loving, encouraging, trusting God; and keep on worshiping together.

One of the most amazing books I have ever read in my life is Ernest Gordon's *Through the Valley of the Kwai*. Ernest Gordon writes about his experience as a prisoner of war in Thailand during World War II. He tells about how the Christmas of 1942 was so radically different from the Christmas of 1943. In 1942, the prisoners were selfish and self-centered. They robbed the sick and mistreated one another. They didn't care whether the other prisoners lived or died. But during the following year, a healthy American soldier began giving his food to a sick buddy to help him get well. In time, the sick prisoner recovered, but the buddy who had given him food died of malnutrition.

The story of the man who gave his life for his friend made the rounds of the camp. Some of the prisoners began to talk about how Christlike that was. They remembered verses of Scripture they had learned years ago under very different circumstances. After that, some of them began to live in the caring spirit of Christ, and the whole prison camp was transformed.

They built a church in the jungle. They had Bible studies. They prayed together. They built a hospital where they could care for the sick, and make medicines from the plants, and make crutches from the trees for those who needed them. They started caring for one another and helping one another. The entire spirit of the camp changed from despair to hope, from selfishness to compassion. And when Christmas of 1943 came, two thousand prisoners gathered for worship. They sang carols and read the story of Christ's birth; but more, they shared their food, and they shared the love of Christ with one another—all because one man came into that prison camp and lived his faith. They were reconciled, made new, socially healed, made one family, all because one man lived in a way that reminded them of the caring spirit of Jesus Christ.

Caring has the power to heal us physically and socially.

In the golden days of the settling of the West, you will remember, of course, that one of the major means of public transportation was the stagecoach. But did you know that in stagecoach days, they had three different kinds of tickets you could buy—first class, second class, and third class?

A first-class ticket meant that you got to sit down. No matter what happened, you could remain seated. If the stagecoach got stuck in the mud or had trouble making it up a steep hill, or even if a wheel fell off, you remained seated, because you had a first-class ticket.

A second-class ticket meant that you got to sit down until there was a problem, and then you had to get off the stagecoach and stand to the side until the problem was resolved. You stood to the side and watched somebody else fix the problem. When the situation was corrected, you could get back on the stagecoach and take your seat, because you had a second-class ticket.

A third-class ticket meant that you got to sit down until there was a problem, and then you had to get off and push! You had to put your shoulder to it and help solve the problem if you had a third-class ticket.

As I thought about this recently, I realized something: I realized that these are precisely the ways in which people relate to the church.

Some think they have a first-class ticket, and they just sit there and expect to be catered to and waited on and pampered.

Others think they have a second-class ticket. They ride along until there is a problem. Then they bail out and become detached spectators. They get off, stand to the side, and watch somebody else fix it.

Still others (and thank God for them) think they have a third-class ticket. They ride along until something goes wrong, and then they get off and push! They address the problem creatively, they work on the situation productively, and they help fix it. They give their energy to the immediate task of solving the problem. They roll up their sleeves and get the job done.

Some years ago at St. Luke's, we started a new Sunday school class for special needs adults who need special education. Most of the class members live in an assisted-living center in Southwest Houston, and we send a van to pick them up and bring them to Sunday school and church every Sunday. They have made a treasured place for themselves in our St. Luke's family. They love to come here, and we love having them here. We named them the Joy Class, and they are well-named because they are a joy.

When we first started the class, there was a young man in the group named Sammy. Sammy came every Sunday, but he did not participate in the class at all. He seemed sad and suspicious, so he withdrew. He sat all by himself in the corner and stared at the floor. He would not sit at the table with the others. He would not eat the refreshments. He would not sing the songs. He would not speak to anybody or look at anybody. No matter how we tried, we could not connect with Sammy. We coaxed and reasoned and pleaded, but with no luck. Sammy would do absolutely nothing except sit in the corner all by himself and stare at the floor.

And then one day, everything changed, and it happened in the most unusual way. A volunteer in our church named Bill would go up to the Joy Class a few times each month to lead their song time. The class members really enjoyed singing, and Bill would play his banjo and sing songs with the class. They all loved it, except Sammy over in his corner. The class would sing songs such as "Jesus Loves Me," "Amazing Grace," " The Old Rugged Cross," "Sweet Hour of Prayer." All would sing along enthusiastically with Bill and his banjo, except Sammy.

Then one day, who knows why, Bill started playing his banjo and singing "Skip to My Lou." Bill had not planned to sing "Skip to My Lou" that morning. It just bubbled out of him. And then the most amazing thing happened. Sammy jumped up out of his chair and did something no one in the class had ever seen him do before: he broke into a big smile! And then for the very first time, Sammy left his corner! He started skipping around the room, laughing and singing "Skip to My Lou" at the top of his voice. When the song was over, Sammy stopped skipping around the room, and he sat down at the table with the others! He joined the group! The class members and leaders were so excited, they all hugged him and welcomed him and patted him lovingly on the back. Sammy smiled broadly and from that point forward, he joyously and enthusiastically participated in everything the Joy Class did, right up until the time he moved away with his family to another city.

There was something about that song, "Skip to My Lou," that somehow touched something deep within Sammy and let him know that the Joy Class was a good thing for him. And from that point, he joined in and loved the class.

We were mystified and curious. We investigated and found that Sammy had loved his grandmother deeply and had lived with her right up until the time of her death. The day after her funeral, he was moved to the center in Southwest Texas. We also found out that when Sammy was a little boy, he would walk to Sunday school and church with his grandmother, and all the way there and back as they walked, he and his grandmother would sing "Skip to My Lou."

That song reminded him of the love and acceptance and joy he knew at church with his grandmother. When Bill and the class began singing that on that pivotal Sunday morning, Sammy suddenly realized that he was in Sunday school and church, and he then knew with confidence that this was a good place for him to be.

That experience gave Sammy a new relationship with the Joy Class and a new relationship with God. All of a sudden, the class became for Sammy a beautiful place and a beautiful group, the symbol of God's acceptance of him and God's love for him. The light bulb turned on, and Sammy realized, "This is church, and I'm loved here and valued here and treasured here!"

During the Great Depression, a group of leaders gathered in Chicago to address the burdensome problems facing the people of our nation. These leaders went to an African American church on the South Side of Chicago. People from the neighborhood came in to discuss their woes and problems as they tried to survive the Great Depression—no jobs, little money, big bills, sagging morale.

Among the leaders who went to see how they might help were a prominent theologian and a famous agnostic attorney. The attorney decided to take advantage of the situation to dramatically underscore the plight of African Americans. He said to them, "You have no jobs; you have no money; you have no power; you have no opportunity." And then he ended by saying, "And yet you sing. No one can sing like you do! There's something I don't understand and I want to ask you about it. What in the world do you have to sing about?"

There was silence in the room, and then the voice of an elderly African American woman came from somewhere in the back of the hall: "We've got Jesus to sing about!" Oh, yes, we have lots of problems, but we also have Jesus and he is what we sing about. For once in his life, the attorney was stopped dead in his tracks. He was face-to-face with people who had faith and hope in Jesus.

CHAPTER EIGHT

STORIES OF BECOMING LIKE CHRIST

In Keith Miller's book *A Second Touch* ([Waco: Word Books, 1967], pp. 63-64) there is a story about a busy executive in an Eastern city who was rushing to catch a commuter train one morning. The executive had an important meeting at the office, and he needed to make this train in order to get there on time. Just as he was about to board the train, he accidentally bumped into a little boy who was carrying a boxed jigsaw puzzle. The box went flying, and the pieces scattered everywhere. What should he do? Should he stop and help the little boy pick up the pieces? Or should he get on the train? He couldn't do both; there was not enough time! If he stopped to help, he would miss the train and be late. What should he do? What would you have done?

Well, the man stopped and helped the boy pick up the puzzle as the train pulled out. The little boy watched him closely with a kind of awe. The little boy said, "Mister, you missed your train."

"I know," the man said.

"Will you be late for work?" the boy asked.

"Yes, but it was more important that I stop and help you."

Then the little boy said, "Mister, can I ask you a question?"

"Yes, of course."

"Mister, are you *Jesus*?"

Keith Miller wrote, "And for the moment, the man realized that—on that platform—he had been." That little boy saw the light of Jesus in that man's act of Christlike love.

Well, how is it with *you* these days? Can people see in you Christ's spirit of forgiveness? And can people see in you Christ's spirit of love?

My father died when I was twelve. As we stood by my dad's casket in the funeral home, hundreds of people came by—all different kinds of people. Some were rich, some were poor, some were young, and some were old. Some were African Americans, some were Anglo Americans, some were Asian Americans, some were Latin Americans, some were professional people, some were uneducated laborers, some were unemployed, some I knew quite well, and some I had never seen before. But they all came. They came over and spoke to us and expressed their sympathy—and every one of them said the same thing to me: "Jim, your dad was kind to me."

Now, they didn't all use those exact words, but each one in his or her own way said the same thing: "Jim, your dad was kind to me." Even though I was just twelve years old at the time, I made up my mind then and there that the best tribute I could pay to my dad was to take up his torch of kindness, to somehow with the help of God let his kindness live on in me, to keep his special brand of kindness alive and well in the world through me, to pass his kindness on to everybody I meet—and from that moment I have tried my best to be a kind person. There are a lot of things I'm not, but since that day I have tried, as a tribute to my earthly father and my heavenly Father, to be a kind person. I haven't always succeeded, but I have tried and I am still trying to let my father's kindness live on in me. You see, I know what kindness is because Wendell Moore was my father! And I have learned even more what kindness is because Jesus Christ is my Savior. The best tribute I can pay my dad and the best tribute I can pay my Christ is to keep their spirit of kindness alive and well in this world.

Every couple is incompatible. You ask anybody who has lived with a married partner for even a few years, and they will tell you that there are incompatibilities with every couple. But love means rising above those things—caring for one another in spite of those things. It means communication and negotiation and compromise and commitment and forgiveness and patience and understanding and kindness. It means giving the other person permission to be who they are—and not trying to force our way on them. It means unconditional love!

I was leading a marriage workshop some years ago. I asked this question: "How do you know your mate loves you?" One woman in the group gave an interesting answer. She said, "You're going to laugh when I tell you this, but I know my husband loves me because he gets me to the airport two hours before my scheduled flight." She was right. Everybody laughed, but she continued, "I know that sounds stupid, but I fly a lot in my business and I have this morbid fear that I'm going to miss my plane, and I want to get there two hours early. I know that's ridiculous and my husband knows it's ridiculous, but he does it. He gets me there because he knows it's important to me, and that's how I know he loves me!"

If you see what looks like a perfect marriage, you can know that a lot of that kind of sacrifice is going on in that relationship because real love knows that there are no perfect people and there are no perfect marriages.

We may be heading toward a spiritual breakdown when we have difficulty praying or studying the Scriptures or making it to church; when we have trouble doing God's will or trusting God, being grateful to God or inspired by God—these are all clear symptoms of "soul sickness."

There is a story often told about Coach Bear Bryant. When Bryant was the football coach at Alabama, his team was winning an important game by four points. But in the fourth quarter, with only forty seconds left in the game, the Alabama quarterback was hurt and had to be helped off the field.

Coach Bryant called for his second-string quarterback and said to him, "Now, son, we have a four-point lead with forty seconds left. I want you to get in there and run out the clock. Don't hand the ball off. Don't pass the ball. Just roll out to the right, run off as much time as you can, and when you sense you are about to be tackled, just go down and hang on to the ball."

With those instructions, the young quarterback ran into the game. He called the play, took the snap, and rolled out to his right. But then he saw his wide receiver wide open downfield, and the quarterback thought to himself, "I've never completed a pass in a college game." And he couldn't resist the temptation. So he threw it! But just as he was letting it go, he was hit from behind and the ball squirted up in the air.

It was intercepted by the fastest cornerback in the Southeastern Conference, who started swiftly down the sideline for what could be the winning touchdown for the other team. But suddenly, the Alabama quarterback who had thrown the errant pass (against Coach Bryant's instructions) got up and started to chase the speedy cornerback. Unbelievably, incredibly, miraculously, he caught him and tackled him at the five-yard line, just as the horn sounded. Alabama had won the game—much to the relief of the quarterback.

After the game, the other coach congratulated Coach Bryant: "I can't believe your quarterback caught my man. He is one of the fastest runners in the United States. I don't know how in the world he caught him."

"Well, it's really very simple," said Coach Bryant. "Your man was running for a touchdown. My man was running for his life!" It's amazing what you can do when you are properly motivated!

Now, if a young football player can be that powerfully motivated by fear of his coach, why can't we turn the coin over and be that powerfully motivated by our confidence in God, our trust in God, our faith in God?

Not long ago, I was watching a late-night TV talk show. The host was interviewing a man whose name you would recognize immediately if I were to state it. He is known all over the world as one of the greatest golfers of all time. He is a world-famous sports figure. He made an interesting confession on TV that night. He said, "I have never been what you'd call a real church-going Christian, but I do consider myself a religious man. When I was a little kid, four years old, my mother taught me a bedtime prayer, and I still say that same prayer today. It's the only one I know."

You know, that seemed kind of sad to me because that is not what happened in other areas of his life. As he grew older and stronger, he did not continue to play golf as he did when he was a "little kid." I should say not! Through hard work, practice, effort, discipline, sacrifice, and commitment, he became one of the superstar golfers in the history of sports. He became one of the finest athletes to ever walk on the face of the earth. But at the age of fifty-two, he is still repeating the same prayer he learned as a child of four. His prayer life had never grown, never stretched, never matured. It was static. There was no development at all. There is something disheartening about that, isn't there?

On September 23, 1930, early in the morning a baby boy was born in Albany, Georgia. At that moment, of course, his family had no way of knowing that this bouncing baby boy would grow up to become one of the most beloved and respected entertainers of all time. He had to triumph over numerous hardships and tragedies along the way, but he did it with style and grace.

When the boy was five years old, he became gravely ill and gradually began to lose his eyesight. By the age of seven he was completely blind. Undaunted, the boy soon learned Braille, and a few years later he began to develop his musical talent by learning to play the piano. When he was fifteen, he became an orphan. Think of that: He was blind, he was orphaned, and he was only fifteen years old. But despite all of that, he refused to give up and give in. He kept working with his music and developing his talent.

At age seventeen, he moved to Seattle, where he organized a musical trio, and he began performing. In 1952, at the age of twenty-two, he signed a recording contract with Atlantic Records and ultimately became a world-famous recording artist and performer. This man's name (of course) is Ray Charles. If you ever saw Ray Charles perform, I'm sure you noticed immediately his creative genius, his soulful energy, his heartfelt sensitivity, his joy in performing the music. He and the music became one. The music seemed to flow freely out of him, and it seemed to come from deep, deep within.

Once, Ray Charles was being interviewed on television by Bob Costas. Bob Costas said to him, "Ray, not too long ago I watched you perform two different concerts on successive nights, and in both concerts you sang your classic hit 'Georgia' but each time you sang it, you did it differently."

Ray Charles replied, "That's right! Every time, I do it differently, because, you see, I don't learn music by notes. I just let it bubble out of my soul!"

Now, when I heard Ray Charles say that, my mind darted back

to a conversation I had participated in a few years ago. A group of people were sitting around one evening after dinner, talking about the great musical entertainers of our time, when someone said, "What is it about Ray Charles that makes him so special?" A man in the group gave an answer that I loved. He said, "Some folks feel the rain; others just get wet. Ray Charles feels the rain!"

Some folks feel the rain; others just get wet. What does that mean? It means that some folks are vividly aware of what's going on around them; they are tuned in, they are sensitive, receptive, responsive, they lead with their hearts, they feel the joy, and they triumph over the pain. But, sadly, many people today don't! They don't celebrate; they just cope. They don't enjoy; they just endure. They don't feel gratitude; they just gripe and grumble. They don't embrace life; they just stonewall through it.

Some folks feel the rain; others just get wet. In other words, some folks smell the roses; others complain about the thorns. Some folks bask in the glow of a beautiful sunset; others dread the darkness that will follow it. Some folks see our time on this earth as a gracious gift from God; others see it as an agonizing endurance test. Some folks seize the day and celebrate life; others just cope.

When Thomas Jefferson was president of our nation, he came one day with a group of friends to a swollen river. They were on horseback, riding cross-country. At the riverbank was a hitch-hiker, a man on foot who couldn't get across the swollen stream. He was standing there trying to catch a ride, trying to find somebody who would transport him across the river.

When President Jefferson and his party rode up, this hitch-hiker went straight over to the President and asked for a ride across the stream. Jefferson reached down, grabbed him by the arm, and pulled him up on the horse behind him. Together they forded the stream, and he then let him off on the other side.

An onlooker came over and, with an amazed look, said to the hitchhiker, "Out of all those men, why in the world did you ask the President to bring you across the river?"

The man answered, "I didn't know he was the President. I just knew he had a 'yes' face!"

The Bible tells us again and again that God has a "yes" face, and he wants us to say yes to life. I find in my own life that when I begin to harbor negative feelings, it is a red flag, a warning signal, that I am getting away from God and losing faith, heading for a spiritual breakdown.

Some years ago, one of our finest church members died. His name was George. Everybody loved George because he was a peacemaker. He had a big heart and a wonderful sense of humor. He used to say that he was so tenderhearted that he cried at supermarket openings! He worked at Methodist Hospital, and he was deeply loved both at church and at work because he was so kind and respectful toward every person he met.

A few days before George died, the president of Methodist Hospital stopped by George's hospital room to see him. They had a nice visit. As the hospital president left, one of the hospital janitors came in to see George. They too had a good visit. When the janitor left, one of George's children said to him, "Dad, did you realize that you treated the president of the hospital and the janitor just alike?" George smiled, and with a chuckle he said, "Let me ask you something. If the president left for two weeks and the janitor left for two weeks, which one would you miss the most?"

But then George said to his children, "Come over here and let me show you something that I carry in my pocket all the time. Even when I mow the lawn, I have these two things in my pocket." With that, he pulled out his pocket cross and his Golden Rule marble. He said, "On the cross are written these words: 'God loves you'; and on the marble are these words: 'Do unto others as you would have them do unto you.'" And then George said, "The cross reminds me of how deeply God loves me, and the marble reminds me of how deeply God wants me to love others."

What George was saying was this: "This is my position, my life stance, symbolized by a little silver cross and a red Golden Rule marble. I just want to let the love of God flow through me and out to others."

That's what it means to be a peacemaker.

Some years ago, there was a great professor at Centenary College named Dean R. E. Smith. Dean Smith was a saintly man, a brilliant scholar, an outstanding communicator, and a real friend to the students. He was a legend in his own time. In one of his most famous lectures, Smith would talk to the students about how we discover truth, how we determine what is genuine and what is false. After some discussion, he would suddenly ask the students this question: "How wide is my desk?" The students would look at the desk and then make their best guesses. A variety of answers would ring out.

"I think it's about seventy-two inches wide."

"No, I believe it's more like sixty-eight inches wide."

"Looks like seventy-five to me."

"I'm going to guess seventy-four."

Then some wise guy from the back of the room would say, "Seventy-one and five-sixteenths," and everybody would laugh. Then Smith would say, "Those are all pretty good guesses, but one of them is more nearly true than the others. Now, how do we determine which one is more accurate? How do we decide which answer is most nearly right and true?" There would be silence in the classroom for a moment and then tentatively someone would suggest, "Get a measuring stick?" "That's right," Smith would say. "To determine which answer is closest to the truth, we have to get a measuring stick and measure." Then Smith would go to the blackboard. He would take a piece of chalk and in silence he would draw the outline of a cross. With that piece of chalk, he would trace over and over the sign of the cross, letting it dramatically sink into the hearts and minds of those students. Then he would stand back and point to that cross and say, "There's your measuring stick! There's your measuring stick for truth!"

Now, look with me at that cross. There's our compass. There's our guiding light. There's our measuring stick for truth. We can put our confidence in that. If the world tries to tell you that it's OK to take advantage of others for your own personal gain; if the world tries to tell you that it's not so bad to lie, cheat, hurt, hold a grudge, or hate; you remember the cross. Remember the truth of Christ.

Have you heard the old story about the wife who became concerned about her husband's health? He was a physical wreck, weak and pale and flabby, stressed out, and constantly tired—totally out of shape. So she took him to the doctor for a check-up.

When the examination was completed, the doctor came out to the waiting room and said to the wife, "Thelma, I just don't like the way your husband looks."

She said, "Neither do I, but he is good to the children!"

Now, believe it or not, there is a point to that story, and here it is: The inner life is more important than outward appearance. Jesus believed that. He talked about that a lot. He was supremely interested in the inner life. The Great Physician was vastly interested in the health of our souls.

In fact, he was so concerned about it that his toughest words were spoken to those who looked good outwardly but were sick within: "Woe to you, scribes and Pharisees...for you are like whitewashed tombs, which outwardly appear beautiful, but within they are full of dead men's bones" (Matthew 23:27). These are stark words.

He also said: "Woe to you, scribes and Pharisees...for you cleanse the outside of the cup and the plate, but inside you are full of greed and wickedness." Hard words!

And, "Beware of false prophets who come to you in sheep's clothing, but inwardly are ravenous wolves." Again, firm words.

Well, what are we to make of this? Why did Jesus speak so strongly about this? Well, it's because he realized that the single most destructive disease, the single most devastating illness, is the sickness within—the sickness in the soul. A hymn writer who understood the importance of this once wrote these words: "It is well with my soul." Can you say that? Is it well with your soul? Is your soul alive and well and close to God? Or is your soul sick and in need of healing?

Recently, I read in a magazine about a college student who, on his first day on campus, was asked to write a theme on the story of his life. A few days later, the professor returned the student's paper graded C+. The student was irate about his grade and protested immediately. "What right," he demanded, "do you have to rate my life a C+?"

Now, I'm sure the professor had other things in mind when he gave that student his grade. But the truth is that many people do indeed have C+ lives.

Remember the old story about the man who went to a psychiatrist and complained that he had an inferiority complex. The psychiatrist tested him and announced, "Well, I have good news and bad news for you. The good news is that you *don't* have a complex; the bad news is that you *are* inferior!"

All of us feel inferior at times. But it helps to remember this: It isn't what we have, but the way we use what we have that makes life count.

Don't miss this point in Jesus' parable of the talents: When the two-talent servant used what he had, even though it was limited, even though it was less than another, his satisfaction from the fulfilled trust was equal to the reward received by the one who got far more in the beginning.

The point is that you can gain as much joy using to the fullest what you have as the fellow who has everything gains from using his.

━━ᴜᴜ┌ᴖ━ ━ᴜᴜ┌ᴖ━ ━ᴜᴜ┌ᴖ━ ━ᴜᴜ┌ᴖ━ ━ᴜᴜ┌ᴖ━

Joy, laughter, and humor are a part of our Scripture and our Christian faith. It's helpful and healthy to laugh at ourselves and the little ironies of life.

Some years ago, Wilsie Martin was appointed as the pastor of a large metropolitan church in Los Angeles. He was honored to receive that prestigious appointment. On his first Sunday to preach, he arrived early. As he stood looking out his study window, he noticed an elderly woman with a walking cane trying to climb the steep front steps to the sanctuary doors. Wilsie Martin rushed out to help her. "Pardon me, ma'am, but could I assist you up these steps this morning?"

"Oh, that would be so kind of you," she answered.

Slowly, tediously, the two climbed together, moving up the steps with great effort to the great doors of the sanctuary entrance. When they finally reached the top, the woman turned to Wilsie and said, "By the way, can you tell me who is preaching at my church this morning?"

"I surely can," came the reply. With his shoulders straight and his head thrown slightly back, he said, "Wilsie Martin is preaching at your church today."

"Oh," said the woman. "Then could you please help me back down the stairs!"

I like that story for two reasons: First, it's funny. But I like it even more for another reason, namely this: How do we know this story? The only way we *could* is because Wilsie Martin told it on himself! He was big enough to laugh at himself, big enough to not

132

take himself too seriously. I'm convinced that our world would be a better place if we would all "lighten up" a bit. If we want to feel the rain and not just get wet, if we want to smell the roses and celebrate life, then we need a sense of gratitude and a sense of humor.

I remember the precise moment when I learned the difference between celebrating life and coping with life. I was in my middle year of seminary. It was the start of the fall semester. I had heard lots of horror stories about this new professor who had come to campus to teach us philosophy of religion. Dr. Williams was his name. He had come from the philosophy department at Ohio State, and he was known far and wide as an excellent teacher but also a stern, tough, unbending taskmaster.

When Dr. Williams handed out the syllabus outlining the course requirements, I couldn't believe my eyes. It called for an incredible amount of reading, a midterm and a final exam, four quizzes, a research project, and six (count them) term papers. After class, I followed Dr. Williams to his office. (Seminary "middlers" are a lot like college sophomores: I thought I knew everything!) I planned to question Dr. Williams about his syllabus and all of those requirements, and to give him a piece of my mind.

I strode into his office. He could tell I was upset. In the most sarcastic tone I could muster, I said to him, "Dr. Williams, you do *realize* that we have other courses besides *yours*, don't you?"

He looked over the top of his glasses and said to me, "Mr. Moore, sit down!" Now, when a professor looks sternly over his glasses at you and says, "Mr. Moore, sit down," you know right away that you are in big trouble! Humbly I sat down and waited for the onslaught.

"Mr. Moore, are you concerned about these six papers that you have to write?" he asked.

"Yes, sir."

"Mr. Moore, are you going to be a pastor?"

"Yes, sir."

"Mr. Moore, are you aware of the fact that you are going to have to write a paper every week for the rest of your life?"

"Sir?"

"Well, out there in the parish they call it a *sermon*, and you've got to write one *every week for the rest of your life*, and I'm going to let you practice on me."

Then came the part that changed my life. Dr. Williams came around from behind his big desk. He took off those ominous-looking glasses and tossed them aside. He sat down beside me, and his tone softened: "You know, Jim [notice he didn't call me *Mr. Moore* this time], you may be going about this all wrong. Don't see these papers and tests as a chore to be done. See them as an opportunity to speak out . . . to say what's on your mind . . . to stand tall for what you believe. Every day, I talk to you; here's your chance to talk to me. Every day, I teach you; look at those papers and tests not as a burden or chore, but as your chance to teach *me*. It's really very simple," he said. "You can celebrate life or cope with life. You can live or vegetate. You can see everything that comes your way as an opportunity or as a burden." And then Dr. Williams said this: "When you get out of school and get in the pastorate, you have a crucial choice to make. Each week you can say, 'Oh God, I have to write a sermon!' Or you can say, 'Thank God, I get to write a sermon!'"

You know what Dr. Williams was saying to me? He was saying something that changed my life forever. He was saying, "Some folks feel the rain; others just get wet. Some folks smell the roses; others gripe about the thorns. Some folks embrace life; others just see it as an endurance test. But as for you, Jim, I want you to feel the rain, smell the roses, embrace and celebrate life!"

Dr. Williams was right because he was underscoring what the psalmist was trying to teach us long ago when he said, "This is the day that the LORD has made; let us rejoice and be glad in it" (Psalm 118:24). These magnificent words have been used for centuries as an appropriate call to worship, but they are so much more. They are also practical and dynamic words for daily living. If you and I could repeat that verse at the beginning of each day (and really mean it), it would change our lives. This is the day that the Lord has made and given to me, as a gracious and precious gift; I will rejoice and be glad in it, and be thankful for it. To resent the day—or to waste the day or to corrupt the day or to curse the day—is sinful and destructive.

How is it with you right now? How are you doing? Are you feeling the rain or just getting wet?

Some years ago, a brilliant and yet eccentric mathematics professor assigned to his students an incredibly difficult math problem for homework. The next day he asked some of the students to go to the board and write out their solutions to the intricate problem. One student after another went to the blackboard, and when they finished their computations the professor simply stated, "No, I'm sorry. That's wrong. Please be seated."

Finally, one student was left. He had worked all night on this math problem. He walked up and wrote his answer on the board. The professor once again said, "That's wrong! Someone else put that answer up there earlier. Didn't you hear me say before that it was wrong?"

"Yes, sir, I did," replied the student, "but it's not wrong. This is the correct answer."

But the professor fired back at him, "That is not the correct answer. I'm sorry. You are wrong. Take your seat."

And the student said, "Sir, I'll be happy to be seated. But with all due respect, I must tell you that you are wrong. This is the correct answer."

The professor looked at him intently and asked, "Are you sure?"

"Yes, sir," answered the student. "I am absolutely sure."

Then the professor smiled and said, "Well, you are right. It is the correct answer!" Then the professor turned to the others in the class and said, "People are looking for solutions today. And they want to be sure that those who provide the solutions have total confidence in them. This young man demonstrated today not only that he knows, but also that he *knows* that he knows!"

That's the kind of confidence we need as Christians these days, isn't it? And we can have it because of God's greatest promise. That great promise is underscored over and over in the Bible— the promise that God will never desert us. He will always be there for us. So, we can do our best and trust God for the rest.

※ ※ ※ ※ ※

In *Fiddler on the Roof*, there is a poignant scene where Tevye, the main character, keeps asking his wife, "Do you love me?" She keeps brushing the question aside by talking of how she has lived with him for so many years. Yet Tevye persists: "But do you love me?" His wife, Golde, talks about how she has worked side by side with him and kept the house. Again Tevye asks, "But do you love me?" Again Golde sidesteps the question by reminding him of how she has borne his children and reared them. But Tevye is not satisfied. He sees his daughters growing up, courting, marrying, and now suddenly the feeling of love runs strong within him. He wants to hear it; he needs to hear it. He wants his wife to say it out loud. He needs reassurance; he wants to know that it is still the same with them. He needs to hear the words *I love you.*

It's presumptuous of us to assume that people know we love them and appreciate them if we never tell them. Husband and wife live together day-in and day-out; surely they love each other, but has it been said lately? Father and son, mother and daughter, sister and brother, living together under the same roof; surely they love one another, but how long has it been since it was said?

Christian friends live next to one another, serve in the same church, share the same pew, sing in the same choir, study in the same Sunday school class. Surely they love one another, but has it been said? Has it been expressed? Has it been verbalized?

Neighbors across a backyard fence, partners across an office desk; we presume our friends know that we love them and appreciate them, but still the question rings out: Has it been said? Have we told them? Have we told them lately?

CHAPTER NINE

SCRIPTURE STORIES

How did you treat your neighbor; how did you treat other people? That is the question we are accountable to answer before God. Sometime, somewhere, that is a key question that will measure and judge our lives. Now we see that documented again here in this graphic parable in Luke 16, the parable of Dives, the rich man, and Lazarus, the poor beggar. It's important to note that this parable is not a geographical description of heaven and hell. It's a drama! It's like a one-act play with two scenes.

Scene 1 opens on an elegant dining room. The table is covered with food and graced with silver candlesticks. Dressed in luxurious purple splendor, Dives, the rich man (we know his name from tradition, though he is not named in the Scriptures), sits there selfishly eating, indulging himself, unaware of and unconcerned about a world out there that may be hurting or hungry. Thus he eats and lives every day. Seated at the door is a poor, wretched beggar, the picture of misery and abject poverty, skin and bones, eyes sunk back, covered with sores.

His name is Lazarus. The unclean street dogs come and lick his sores, and he is so weak that he cannot ward them off or run them away. Lazarus is waiting for the bread that will be thrown his way from the rich man's table. Scholars tell us that in those days, people didn't have napkins, so they wiped their lips and chins and fingers with bread and then threw the bread aside. This was what Lazarus was waiting for, the thrown-away bread, as scene 1 comes to an end.

As the curtain goes up on scene 2, the tables are turned. The roles are completely reversed. Lazarus (the poor beggar) has now died and is in comfort in heaven, while Dives is in agony in hell. Dives, the rich man, pleads that Lazarus might be sent to earth as a miraculous messenger from the dead to warn his five brothers. But the answer comes back that the brothers have Moses and the prophets to look to for guidance, and that if they don't hear them, then they won't be convinced by someone rising from the dead. With that pronouncement the curtain closes, and the play ends.

But what does it mean? What do we make of this? What can we learn from this? What is Jesus trying to teach us here? That it's wrong to be rich? Of course not! We miss the point if we come to that conclusion. The sin of Dives was not in being wealthy. His sin was in not caring. His sin was his blind self-centeredness. His sin was his arrogant, indulgent apathy.

This is a tremendously relevant parable for our time because "the Dives Syndrome" is so dramatically with us today in what is called the epidemic of "me-ism." Go to the bookstore this week and notice the great number of books (many of them on the best-seller charts) that propose trendy techniques to get the most pleasure, power, and personal satisfaction out of life. The theme of many of these books is "meism"—"look out for number one" or "power by intimidation." The Dives Syndrome is still with us, extolling the virtues of selfishness.

At the first Pentecost, the disciples were waiting there in Jerusalem, not really sure what they were supposed to do next. They were confused and fuzzy. Their vision was clouded and uncertain. They wanted and needed help. They wanted the Holy Spirit to come and open their eyes, and that is exactly what happened. Remember the story with me.

Christ has been crucified. He has risen and appeared to the disciples. He has told them that he must leave them but that he will not leave them alone. He will send a comforter, a counselor. The Holy Spirit will come and be with them and give them power and courage and vision, and they will take up Christ's ministry and be his witnesses to all the world.

Jesus has ascended into heaven, and the disciples have returned to the Holy City to wait for the Holy Spirit. Now, here they are waiting and wondering, not sure how all of this is going to turn out, not sure just what they are supposed to do next.

They don't fully understand all that has happened. They don't see clearly what their task is yet. They sit there waiting—waiting and wondering. Then suddenly on the day of Pentecost they hear a sound—the rush of a mighty wind—the breath of God is blowing on that place. Immediately, they are all filled with the Holy Spirit, and they begin to speak out in other tongues. Now, don't mistake this for the unknown tongues. They are speaking in the languages of people of all the nations.

People hear the sounds and come running. A great crowd (thousands of people) assembles there, representing all the nations of the world—Asians, Arabians, Egyptians, Italians, Parthians, Medes, and Elamites.

Folks from everywhere, all nations and countries, gather, and they are amazed because each one of them hears his or her own native tongue being spoken. Someone in the crowd, bowled over by this communications miracle, cries out, "What can this mean?"

But then some cynic answers (there's one in every crowd). The cynic says, "Aw, they're just drunk!"

Now, this is the moment Simon Peter has been waiting for. He sees it all clearly now. The Holy Spirit has opened his eyes to see that Christ was not just a Jewish Messiah, but more, the Savior of the world, the Lord of all people and all nations. Peter sees it now, and now he knows what he is supposed to do.

Simon Peter stands up, and he begins to speak: "No! These men are not drunk. The Spirit of God is upon them, and they realize now the truth of God as never before. Jesus of Nazareth, the one you crucified: God has raised him up! He has appeared to us. He is the Son of God, the Lord of life, the Savior of the whole world."

When the crowd heard that, they were ashamed of what they had done. They were cut to the heart: "You mean we tried to kill the Son of God! Oh no! What should we do?"

Peter answers, "It's not too late. God, in His grace, will forgive you. Repent and be baptized in the name of Jesus Christ for the forgiveness of your sins, and you too will receive this gift of the Holy Spirit. The promise is open to all. Whosoever will, may come." And the Scriptures tell us that three thousand souls were saved that day.

The powerful story of Pentecost has much to teach us. The point is clear. Through the gift of the Holy Spirit, our hearts are warmed, our spirits are strengthened, and our eyes are opened. The coming of the Holy Spirit into our lives gives us new vision, a new way of looking at things.

Those disciples that Pentecost morning were not drunk. They were not filled with new wine. They were filled with the Spirit of God, and that Holy Spirit opened their eyes to incredible new possibilities.

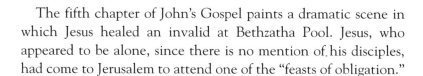

The fifth chapter of John's Gospel paints a dramatic scene in which Jesus healed an invalid at Bethzatha Pool. Jesus, who appeared to be alone, since there is no mention of his disciples, had come to Jerusalem to attend one of the "feasts of obligation."

In biblical times, three Jewish feasts were feasts of obligation: Passover, Pentecost, and Tabernacles. All adult male Jews who lived within fifteen miles of Jerusalem were legally bound to attend these three feasts.

Jesus made his way to the famous pool, where all the people stared with great intensity at the water, waiting expectantly for it to move. Beneath the pool was a subterranean stream that every now and then bubbled up. The belief was that the disturbance was caused by an angel, and the first person to get into the pool after the troubling of the water would be healed.

To us, this may sound like superstition. But it was the kind of belief that was widespread in ancient times. People believed in all kinds of spirits. Every tree, every river, every bush, every hill, every pool, had its resident spirit. Ancient peoples were especially impressed with the power and holiness of water. We may know water only as something that comes out of a faucet, but in the ancient world water was the most valuable, the most powerful, the most awesome of all things. Surely this notion was a factor in the origin of the rite of baptism.

When Jesus walked into that intriguing scene, his eye fell immediately upon a pitiful situation, a man who had been ill for thirty-eight years. All those years he had watched and waited and hoped, and somehow Jesus knew the man had been there a long time.

Notice that Jesus is not pushy here. He doesn't force himself on the man. Tenderly, gently, he asks, "Do you want to be healed?" And when the lame man answers, "Oh yes, but I have no one to help me," Jesus reaches out with love. He does not fuss or argue or lecture. He meets the man where he is. He says, "Get up! Take up your bed and walk!" and the man gets up and walks away— and Jesus gets into trouble for healing on the sabbath.

Now, this fascinating story has, over the years, captured the imagination of poets, preachers, and theologians. All kinds of questions have been raised and analyzed: How did Jesus heal the man? What does the pool symbolize? Did the water really have medicinal powers? What about the Sheep Gate, the porches, the thirty-eight years? the healing on the sabbath? the place of this story in the Gospel of John?

These questions are interesting, but I would like to raise one more: Why didn't somebody help the man? All those years, he had waited. He said, "I have no one to help me." Why not?

Mark 5 tells the story of a woman who had a flow of blood for over twelve years. Under the premise of "We can't be too careful," look at what her society was doing to her. Under the concept of "We can't be too careful," this innocent woman was being shunned and ostracized and abused by society.

She was a battered person, terribly in need of compassion. As far as we know, she had not been battered physically, but without question, she was being battered socially, emotionally, and spiritually by the world in which she lived. They told her she was dirty, and that everything and every person she touched she contaminated and made unclean. It was written into their law. Remember these tough words from Leviticus 15: "When a woman has a discharge of blood that is her regular discharge from her body, she shall be in her impurity for seven days, and whoever touches her shall be unclean. Everything upon which she lies . . . everything also upon which she sits shall be unclean. Whoever touches anything upon which she sits . . . shall be unclean, and shall wash his clothes, and bathe in water, and be unclean until the evening" (vv. 19-27).

Think about that. Her society told her harshly that she was filthy, and that they couldn't be too careful with her. But even worse, they told her that God was angry with her and that he had sent this misfortune on her, because in their minds they believed she had done some terrible thing to displease him. Of course, they were wrong about that, but they laid guilt and shame on her by the bucketsful. She was labeled unclean and treated with contempt. Why? Simply because she was sick, simply because she had this unmentionable problem, simply because she had had this flow of blood for twelve years.

For twelve long years her society had battered her. They wouldn't let her go to parties or to weddings or to the marketplace or to church. They wouldn't let her go anywhere where she might touch another person. They were saying, "You have this embarrassing problem, and we can't be too careful with you." But think of what that kind of treatment would do to you emotionally, mentally, socially, and spiritually. This woman was tremendously in need of a little compassion and a little caring. And then one day, along came Jesus. Let's look at the story in Mark 5 (also told in Luke 8) together.

Jesus was on his way to see a little girl who was critically ill, when suddenly he was interrupted. As he was moving through the streets, people began to press in around him. The New English Bible puts it dramatically: "He could hardly breathe for the crowds" (Luke 8:42). The people were so excited to be near Jesus that they were pushing and shoving and crowding in close to him. This woman who had been hemorrhaging for twelve years wasn't even supposed to be out there in the crowd, but she was desperate, so she was there.

She slipped up behind Jesus, working her way through the crowd, and when no one was looking, she reached out tentatively, fearfully, and touched the hem of his robe. Right then, the story tells us, her bleeding stopped. She thought she had pulled it off. She thought she had gone unnoticed, so she dropped back and tried to lose herself in the huge crowd.

But then, suddenly, Jesus stopped. He turned around and said, "Who touched me?" (see Luke 8:45). The disciples were astonished by the question. "Who touched you? What do you mean, who touched you? *Everybody's* touching you. In this crowd, everybody's touching everybody! What kind of question is that?" But Jesus knew that it was a special touch.

He began to look around. The woman had not expected to be found out, but timidly she stepped forward and told Jesus everything—about this bleeding that had gone on for so long, about how she had tried everything, but nothing had helped, and in fact, she had only gotten worse. She told Jesus that she had heard about him and his power to heal, and how she felt that if she could just touch his clothing, she could be made well. And it had worked. It had worked! The bleeding had stopped.

Jesus' heart went out to her, and he spoke to her tenderly: "Daughter, your faith has made you well; go in peace, and be healed of your disease" (Mark 5:34).

Now, in this fascinating story, we see the compassionate spirit of Jesus, and we discover a crucial lesson for life—that we *can't* be too *caring*, but we *can* be too *careful*.

How long has it been since you had one of those moments that takes your breath away? As we have been reminded in numerous ways in recent years (through billboards, banners, plaques, bumper stickers, church bulletins, and so forth), "It is not the number of breaths we take, it is the number of moments that take our breath away." And this is so true! Life is so much more than an endurance test. It is so much more than "tick-tock time"— time measured by the ticking of a clock, with each second exactly like the one that preceded it and the one that follows it. No, every now and then—and more often than we realize—God breaks into the routine and gives us one of those awesome moments, so powerful, so amazing, so beautiful, that "time seems to stand still." It's a moment that takes our breath away!

This is what happened to Isaiah in the Temple (Isaiah 6). He came to the Temple that day as he had come routinely so many times before, but on that day he "saw the Lord high and lifted up." It took his breath away, and he accepted God's call to be a prophet. He heard God's call, "A prophet is needed for this hour"; and with breathtaking excitement, Isaiah responded, "Here am I; send me" (v. 8).

This is precisely what happened to Moses in Exodus 3. Moses was watching over his father-in-law's flock one day, as he had so many days before, when all of a sudden God appeared to him in a burning bush. Moses was so inspired by that breathtaking moment that he took off his shoes, because he knew this was a sacred moment and he was standing on "holy ground" (v. 5). And from that moment, he set out to go to Egypt and set God's people free.

And look at Jesus. Jesus in his lifetime on earth inspired so many breathtaking moments. All kinds of images come to mind:

- The shepherds and the wise men, kneeling in awe and wonder at the manger;
- The elders in the Temple, amazed and astonished by the wisdom and insight of the twelve-year-old Jesus;
- Zacchaeus, up in a sycamore tree, so bowled over by Jesus' acceptance of him that he comes down out of that tree giving money away;
- Bartimaeus on the Jericho Road, healed of his blindness by Jesus, so inspired by Jesus' goodness and power that he drops everything and follows Jesus on the way;
- The woman in the crowd who touched the hem of Jesus' robe in hopes that this simple gesture could bring the healing she had been seeking for twelve long years; and when the healing does indeed come, she is overwhelmed by the love and power of Jesus in that breathtaking moment;
- Doubting Thomas in the upper room, who finally sees the risen Christ with his own eyes and falls in amazement on his knees, exclaiming, "My Lord and my God!";
- Saul of Tarsus, encountering the resurrected Lord on the Damascus Road, so blown away by God's amazing grace in that breathtaking moment that he is converted and becomes

God's missionary to the Gentiles and the prolific writer of much of what we now call the New Testament.

We could go on and on, because Jesus' life was filled with moments that take our breath away. I am sure that right now you are thinking of many others, because there are so many.

But the question is: How is it with you? How long has it been since you had a moment like that—a moment so powerful, so touching, so awesome, that it took your breath away?

⸺⸺⸺⸺⸺

God's power is available. God's strength is accessible. God's energy is at hand. God's presence is nearer than breathing. God's forgiveness is freely offered. But some lives just are not connected! They live in the shadow of the power source, but they are not plugged in!

We see this dramatically in Jesus' parable of the Pharisee and the publican. Evidently the publican, this tax collector, had had a bad day, maybe one of the worst days of his life, because he was driven by his problems to the Temple, ashamed, groping, sorrowful, remorseful, beating upon his chest.

Catch the agony of that now: "beating upon his chest"—the vivid, dramatic, heart-wrenching symbol of penitence. Jesus tells us that this man, this painfully penitent man, went home justified, rather than the other man. The publican's worst day may have turned out to be his best day, because his worst day brought him back to God. It caused him to plug in to the power of God's grace. While the other, the Pharisee, lived daily in the presence of God (he was a religious professional), somehow he was not connected; he was not plugged into the power source. Remember the story with me.

This story is found only in the Gospel of Luke, and that is fitting because in Luke's Gospel, we see over and over how much

Jesus loved stories with surprise endings, and how much he loved stories where in the end the little guy comes out on top. We see both of those elements in this great parable.

Two men go up to the Temple to pray. One is a Pharisee, and the other is a publican, a tax collector. The Pharisee, the symbol of religious authority in that day, marches proudly in. This is his turf. He is a big man at the Temple. He knows his way around, and he strides in. Using his most arrogant swagger, he marches to the most prominent spot in that sacred place to show off how pious he is. *People will be very impressed with my religiosity, and well they should,* he reasons, and then he prays this prayer: "God, I thank you that I am not like other people: thieves, rogues, adulterers, or even like this tax collector. I fast twice a week [by the way, the law demanded only one fast per week]; I give a tenth of all my income" (Luke 18:11-12). (The law required that only agricultural products be tithed.) So prays the proud Pharisee. But the tax collector, in humility and penitence, stands reverently toward the back of the Temple, far from the altar. He beats upon his chest, ashamed of what he has done. He plugs into the power of God's grace, and he prays for forgiveness: "God, be merciful to me, a sinner!" (v. 13).

Jesus concludes the parable by saying, "I tell you, this man [the humble, penitent tax collector, this man who plugged into the power of God's mercy] went down to his home justified rather than the other" (v. 14), the arrogant Pharisee who relied upon and bragged about his own religious accomplishments. And then Jesus concludes with this statement: "All who exalt themselves will be humbled, but all who humble themselves will be exalted."

One day Jesus told the story about a man who was about to make a trip to a far country. Just before leaving, he called in three of his servants and gave them oversight of his money. To one he gave five talents, to another two talents, and to the last, he gave one talent—and then he left on his journey.

A talent, the largest monetary unit of the day, would have been several years' wages for those servants. The servant with five talents went and traded and gained five more; and the servant with two talents went out and worked and gained two more. But the servant with one talent dug a hole in the ground and hid his master's money because he was afraid he might lose it.

When the master returned, he was delighted with the two servants who had worked and doubled their talents. "Well done, good and trustworthy slave," he said to them. "You have been trustworthy in a few things, I will put you in charge of many things; enter into the joy of your master" (Matthew 25:21). But when the servant with one talent came in and said: "Master, I knew that you were a harsh man, . . . so I was afraid, and I went and hid your talent in the ground. Here you have what is yours" (vv. 24-25).

The master was much displeased. He rebuked the servant, calling him wicked and lazy—and he gave that talent to the one with ten.

Now, what is this story all about? Of course, I know a parable is a story with one central truth, but if I may use poetic language, I would like to point out that there are many fascinating insights here. Let me quickly list a few of them. The parable points out:

1. Mere abstinence from evil is not enough; we must use our talents to do good.

2. If we don't use our gifts, we lose them (ask any musician or athlete or surgeon about that— they know how true that is).

3. Each one of us is unique; every servant receives something, but our talents are different.

4. Life is a sacred trust, and we are accountable to God for it— we are his stewards—we and all we have belong to the master.

5. We are measured not by the amount of our talents, but by what we do with what we have (be sure to notice that the five-

talent servant and the two-talent servant received exactly the same reward).

6. We can easily be tempted to be a loser, to bury our talent, to quit on life, to use littleness as an excuse, to hide behind feelings of inferiority, and to dream of what might have been if only we had been given a little bit more.

Of course, all of these insights are important, but what I want to get to is the question of why the one-talent servant failed. What paralyzed him? What went wrong? Well, he failed because he did nothing but bury his talent. He did nothing because he was afraid! He was literally imprisoned by his own fears.

⟶✦⟵ ⟶✦⟵ ⟶✦⟵ ⟶✦⟵ ⟶✦⟵

Celebrating the giver rather than the gift—that is the key. And when you make that breakthrough, you can never be the same. That kind of gratitude will change your life! There is a beautiful example of this in the Bible: the story of Zacchaeus in Luke 19. Remember the story with me.

Jesus and his disciples are heading toward the showdown in Jerusalem. As they pass through Jericho, they see that a great crowd has gathered to see Jesus. Zacchaeus is in the crowd. The Scriptures tell us that Zacchaeus was a chief tax collector and was rich and that he was disliked and despised by his fellow towns-people. They resented paying taxes to Rome, and they felt that Zacchaeus, a fellow Jew, had betrayed them, had sold out to Rome, and had gotten rich at their expense. So they rejected him, shunned him, detested him. If you had conducted a popularity contest in Jericho that day, Zacchaeus may well have come in dead last.

This was the setting when Jesus came to Jericho that day. People had heard about Jesus and had gathered along the streets to see him. Zacchaeus was also eager to see the Nazarene, but Zacchaeus was short and couldn't see over the crowd. So

Zacchaeus ran ahead and climbed into a sycamore tree in hopes of getting a glimpse of this great leader everyone was talking about.

When Jesus saw him, he sensed that Zacchaeus was the loneliest man in town, and his heart went out Zacchaeus. Jesus looked up and said, "Zacchaeus, make haste, and come down; for to-day I must abide at thy house" (Luke 19:5 KJV). Zacchaeus was visibly touched, indeed, overwhelmed by this acceptance and this special honor. It had been a long time since anyone had been nice to him. Zacchaeus was so grateful, so filled with gratitude, that it changed his life.

Notice that Jesus gave him no material gifts. He gave him something better: love, respect, acceptance, and forgiveness. Zacchaeus became so grateful that his whole lifestyle changed. Why, it even touched his pocketbook. Before he had been a "taker," and he became a "giver."

That's the way it works. When we become truly grateful to God for the gift of his love, we can't be the same anymore! We are changed! We are turned around. We are converted, transformed. Zacchaeus was so grateful for Christ's acceptance of him and love for him that his life, his relationships, and his reason for living were all dramatically changed. That's what real gratitude does! It changes our lives! Let me show you what I mean.

It's still happening. Old men start wars; young men and women have to fight them. We see a classic example of this as far back as early Old Testament times. Way back in 1 Samuel 17, we find the famous and popular story of David and Goliath. There we read about how the small shepherd boy, David, armed only with his trusty slingshot, was sent out to do battle against the most powerful warrior in the Philistine army, a giant of a man named Goliath. Even his name sounds fearsome, doesn't it? Goliath! You wouldn't want to meet him in a dark alley at night.

This famous story celebrates the universal emotion to pull for the underdog. It also marks the beginning of David's meteoric rise to prominence as one of Israel's greatest leaders and heroes.

The Philistines were quite a threat in those days. They were the swaggering military bullies of that time, and they enjoyed kicking sand in the faces of their enemies. They did it with gusto! Because of their monopoly on iron, the Philistines had an edge on everybody. They had superior weapons, extraordinary armor, and better mobility because they could build and use chariots. In addition, they had well-trained, well-disciplined soldiers, who strutted about with bold confidence.

On the other hand, the Israelites were so ill-equipped and so poorly prepared that at first glance any military expert would look at this situation and say, "It's hopeless for the Israelites. They are done for. The party's over. They don't have a chance against the mighty Philistine army." And on top of all that, the Philistines had a not-so-secret weapon—a powerful giant warrior who struck panic into the heart of almost everyone who saw him, a giant soldier who had the Israelites trembling with fear and quaking in their boots.

Goliath, the giant, was so huge that he towered over everybody and so powerful that he carried a spear most men would not be strong enough to throw. And he was covered from head to toe with the finest protective armor available in that day. He looked and sounded invincible as he screamed out his insulting taunts to the smaller, less properly attired Israelites. Goliath was arrogant and ruthless and mean, and the Israelite soldiers were scared to death of him. No one wanted to face the giant Goliath.

But then along came little David, the shepherd boy. David had come to the front lines to bring food and supplies for his older brothers, who were soldiers in the Israelite army. That's the way it worked back then. Since there was no strong central government, there were no K-rations, no C-rations, no MREs (meals ready to eat), no supplies at all. Each soldier had to be fed and equipped by his own family.

Therefore, father Jesse had sent his young son David to the battlefront to bring provisions. Evidently David was too young to join the army and had to stay home with his family, tending the sheep. However, when David arrived at the front and heard the brash, haughty taunts of Goliath, he immediately volunteered to battle the giant.

King Saul hesitated to send this inexperienced young boy out to challenge the mighty giant, but finally the king gave in and consented when he realized David's resolute determination: "David said, 'The LORD, who saved me from the paw of the lion and from the paw of the bear, will save me from the hand of this Philistine.'"

Trying to be helpful, King Saul called for his best armor and put it on David. But that didn't work at all. It was too big, too heavy, too cumbersome, and David could barely move in it. So David said, "Thanks, but no thanks. I can't wear another man's armor. I have to do it my way." He took off the heavy armor and set it aside. And then he went out to face the giant, armed only with a slingshot, five smooth stones, and the absolute confidence that God would go with him and see him through. Armed with that blessed assurance, David was not afraid. Rather, he was poised, courageous, and confident.

Now, when Goliath saw little David, of all people, coming out to face him, the giant warrior was both amused and insulted—amused that so unlikely a foe had the nerve to confront him, and insulted that the Israelites would stoop to sending out a small, inexperienced shepherd boy—with no armor, no sword, no spear—to do battle with him, the most feared warrior of that time. The more Goliath thought about it, the more livid he became, and he felt no sympathy at all for his young opponent. Brashly, the giant moved forward to make quick work of young David.

But David had a surprise for Goliath. With his dependable slingshot, young David struck the giant at his only vulnerable place—right between the eyes, on his forehead—and the giant went down to defeat. When the Philistines saw their champion cut down by a little shepherd boy, they promptly went into a panic and ran away full of fear.

Now, what can we learn from this colorful ancient story? How does it impact our lives today? What does it have to say to you and me right now? What are the timeless lessons here for the living of these days? Well, actually, there are many wonderful insights for us here.

For one thing, we see the importance of facing our fears squarely—not running away from them, but facing them head-on.

And we see the amazing strength and courage that come from a sense of God's presence with us.

⟞⟝ ⟞⟝ ⟞⟝ ⟞⟝ ⟞⟝

One of the Kingdom parables of Jesus in Matthew's Gospel underscores the danger of overreaction. It is traditionally called the parable of the wheat and the tares, or the parable of the weeds among the wheat. In this parable, Jesus is calling for patience, and warning us against hasty, emotional, impulsive, violent action. Be patient! Trust God! Trust the test of time! The truth will come out!

Remember how it goes. Jesus said that the kingdom of heaven is like a man who had sown his field with wheat. He had been very particular about the good quality of the seed. But during the night, the man's enemy came and sowed weeds among the wheat, then slipped away into the darkness. Later the servants went out into the field, where they expected to find a good grain crop. But to their amazement and dismay, they found weeds growing among the wheat! The servants came back and asked the master: "Sir, did you not sow good seed? Where did the weeds come from?" He answered: "An enemy has done this!"

The servants, filled with anger, impulsively wanted to act immediately, explosively, and violently. They wanted to purge the field. They wanted to go out and rip up the weeds and get rid

155

of them right away. But the master was a man of patience and self-control. He said: "No! Let's wait, for if you pull up the weeds now, you might harm the wheat. We will wait and let both grow together, and then I will separate them at the harvest. Then we will get rid of the weeds and gather the wheat into my barn."

Now, there are several interesting observations that can be made from this fascinating parable. Let me mention some of them.

For one thing, the parable reminds us that there are no perfect situations; there are always weeds among the wheat.

The parable also makes it clear that the Master is not responsible for the weeds. He sowed only the best seed, but somehow we have cultivated weeds rather than the Bread of Life.

The parable also underscores the fact that there are some judgments we are not capable of making. They belong to the Master. And it shows that the weeds and wheat may look alike at first, but they are ultimately distinguished by their fruits.

And there is good news here: There will be a harvest. The weeds will not choke out the wheat, so be patient, keep your balance, sow good seed, and trust God to bring it out right.

—⁘— —⁘— —⁘— —⁘— —⁘—

Let's remember together that powerful scene in 1 Kings 18 where the great prophet Elijah says to the people, "How long will you go limping with two different opinions? If the LORD is God, follow him; but if Baal, then follow him" (v. 21). What is this all about? Why did Elijah say that? What on earth is he talking about? Let me try to put it in context for us.

When the people of Israel came into the promised land of Canaan, they settled down beside their Canaanite neighbors. The people of Israel who had been wandering in the wilderness for many years (and had been slaves in Egypt for many years before that) now tried their hand at farming—and they didn't know the first thing about it. They had been nomads. The Canaanites, on the other hand, had been farming for many years. They knew how to do it. The Israelites had never farmed before at all. They were rookies at farming, totally inexperienced.

So when the time came for that first harvest, who do you think had the best crops? Why, the Canaanites, of course, because they were experienced farmers. They knew what they were doing. They knew how to farm. The Israelites went over to their Canaanite neighbors and said, "We notice that your crops are much better than ours. Why is that? How did you do it?"

"Simple," the Canaanites said, "we prayed to Baal! He is our local fertility god, and we pray to him, and he gives us good crops."

Actually, Baal had nothing to do with it, but they *thought* he did. So the Israelites began to wonder and reason like this: "We know God said to us, 'Have no other gods, and make no graven images.' We know we are supposed to worship God alone. But we sure would like to have better crops next year. Maybe if we prayed to Baal, just a little bit . . . what could it hurt? It might even give us a better harvest. Maybe it's worth a try."

But then along came the prophet Elijah. He saw what was happening, and he knew that it was wrong and hurtful and dangerous. He knew that this thinking and these actions were a violation of the Ten Commandments. He knew that Baal worship represented superstition and immorality and idolatry, and he knew he had to stand tall and speak out against this wrongful practice. Elijah also knew he had to do it powerfully, graphically, and convincingly. So he challenged the 450 prophets of Baal to a contest. The question was, Who is in charge of the universe? Is it God? Or is it Baal?

Elijah set up the contest. They piled up wood for a bonfire. Elijah then told the prophets of Baal to call on Baal to miraculously ignite the fire. For hours, the 450 prophets of Baal called out to their god, over and over again, but to no avail: Nothing happened. Elijah chided them, "Maybe you should cry louder. Maybe Baal has gone to sleep. Or maybe he is daydreaming right now. Or maybe he has gone on a trip" (1 Kings 18:27, paraphrased). By the way, the Scriptures tell us that those Canaanite prophets "limped around" their bonfire altar, crying out to Baal louder and louder, but no response, no answer, no fire. Finally, exhausted, they gave up.

Elijah then stepped forward to give it a try. To make the task more difficult and more awesome, Elijah asked that the bonfire wood be doused with water—not once, not twice, but three times! Then Elijah called on God to send fire from heaven—and immediately it came! The Scriptures describe it like this: "The fire of the LORD fell and consumed the burnt offering, the wood, the stones, and the dust, and even licked up the water that was in the trench. When all the people saw it, they fell on their faces and said, 'The LORD indeed is God; the LORD indeed is God'" (1 Kings 18:38-39).

In that ancient contest, the question Elijah put before the people of Israel is the same question we need to face today, namely this: "How long will you go limping with two different opinions? If the LORD is God, follow him; but if Baal, then follow him" (1 Kings 18:21).

Also by James W. Moore

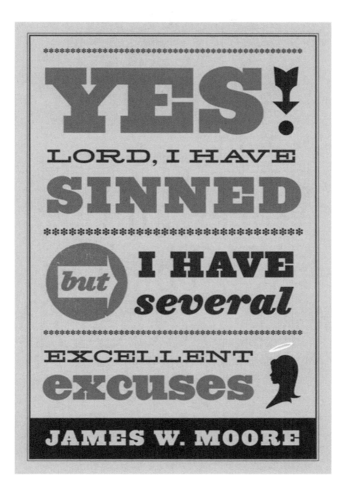

JAMES W. MOORE

I Hear Voices, and That's a GOOD Thing!

JAMES W. MOORE

Do You Have Alligator Arms?

EMBRACING LIFE, HOPE, AND GOD

WHEN
ALL ELSE
FAILS
READ
the
INSTRUCTIONS

JAMES W. MOORE